WATER GARDEN
WORKBOOK

GROUND FORCE

WATER GARDEN WORKBOOK

Charlie Dimmock

BBC

This book is published to accompany the television series entitled *Ground Force*, which was first broadcast in 1997. The series was produced by Bazal (part of GMG Endemol Entertainment) for BBC Television.

Executive Producer: Carol Haslam
Producer/director: John Thornicroft

Published by BBC Worldwide Limited, Woodlands,
80 Wood Lane, London W12 0TT

First published 1999
Reprinted 1999, 2000 (Twice), 2001(Twice), 2002 (Twice), 2004
Copyright © Charlie Dimmock and Bazal
The moral right of the author has been asserted.

ISBN 0 563 55113 5

Commissioning Editor: Nicky Copeland
Project Editor: Rachel Brown
Designer: Isobel Gillan
Illustrator: Amanda Patton
Picture Researcher: Susannah Parker

Set in Gill sans serif and Rotis sans serif
Printed and bound in France by Imprimerie Pollina s.a. - n° L92944
Colour separations by Imprimerie Pollina s.a.
Cover printed by Imprimerie Pollina s.a.

Many of the projects in this book include electrically powered pumps and every effort has been made to recommend the safest way of installing them. When you buy the electrical components for any project, always check that they are designed to be used in water and if in doubt at any stage, seek the advice of a qualified electrician. Advice is also given on child safety and every care has been taken to ensure that this information is correct. It should be noted, however, that children can drown in very shallow depths of water and must not be left unsupervised near a water feature. The publishers and the author cannot accept any legal responsibility or liability for accidents incurred as a result of the construction of any of the projects described in this book.

contents

introduction

I was brought up with ponds around me. My parents always had them in their garden, so it just seemed natural for me to end up working with them. There is a special magic about water, but if you think a pond is all peace and tranquillity, you should take a look at what goes on under the surface. It's like one of those long-running television soaps. There is much more happening in a water garden than in your average herbaceous border, however beautiful. And that's what I love about ponds. As well as beautiful flowers and fabulous foliage, you've got reflections, movement and the sound of babbling water. There are colourful insects darting about, and wild creatures coming to drink and bathe. A pond contains plants with peculiar habits, like the water soldier that sinks to the bottom or floats according to temperature, and a variety of creatures that resemble anything from miniature prehistoric monsters to Martians, all with their own daily dramas. All you have to do is sit back and watch.

Of course, water gardening brings its own sets of rewards and challenges that are quite unlike the normal dry-land sort. For a start you need a different set of skills. A water gardener has to be part plantsman and part plumber. It helps if you are a bit of an artist, handyman and naturalist too. But when it comes to *Ground Force*, you can add another talent: clock-watching. Every garden we make has to be completed in just two days, and, no, we don't have an army of secret helpers who take over our picks and shovels as soon as the camera stops running. Nowadays we can count on Tommy's assistant, Will, and we get the odd bit of help from the family of the 'surprisee' too, but even so time is often *very* tight. I can't tell you how often I've watched a programme and thought, 'We can't possibly do that in the time,' even though I know we did because I was there! So if you fancy trying one

or two of the projects at home, you can afford to do it at your own pace. There's no need to copy them exactly either: just use them as a source of information and ideas. Similarly, treat our prices for the things we used just as a guide. On the programme our budget for each garden is £1000. And though we sometimes exceed this slightly, we get good value for money as, being in the business, we all have our own sources of unusual or recycled materials that you might not be able to find as cheaply in garden centres – and, in any case, prices vary all round the country.

One thing I'm always being asked is: 'Has *Ground Force* changed your life?' The answer is no. I still manage Mill Water Gardens in Romsey, where I first worked as a Saturday girl, and where I have worked ever since I finished horticultural college. It has made me a lot of new friends, though, as people who watch the programme have got to know me and treat me like a pal right from the start, which is great. I get a very different reaction from men too. Now I'm accepted as a sort of honorary builder's labourer.

As I write we've already started work on the next television series, so I hope you'll join us for more spectacular high-speed garden makeovers – I can promise you there are lots of completely new and exciting water features coming up. See you then!

Happy water gardening.

GETTING GOING

before
you start

In a good water garden all you should see are the plants, the fish and the water. As for the technical gubbins that make it all work, you shouldn't know they are there. This is why, if you asked me the secret of successful water gardening, I'd have to say 'advance planning'. Always plan the whole thing on paper first, so you know where you are going to hide your water pipes and electric cables: that way you won't have to dig up the patio or chip holes in your pond surround later.

CHOOSING A WATER FEATURE

You probably already have a mental picture of the sort of water feature you would like – perhaps a formal lily pond, or a wildlife pond alive with dragonflies and frogs. Personal choice plays a big part in the decision, but you need to think about practical considerations too.

Take safety first. Do small children use the garden, or – if you're planning a front garden feature – could they wander in from the street? I consider a water feature fairly child-friendly if the water deepens gradually as in a wildlife pond, or is in a container, where a child cannot step straight into deep water. The only truly child-proof kinds are those that have no standing water, like pebble pools. But even a normal pond can be made more child-friendly by covering the water with a metal grid, hidden by water plants growing through it.

Then there is maintenance. A water feature which does not have any fish or plants needs much less attention than a fully stocked pond, which generates a lot of debris and needs regular attention.

Do you want moving water, such as a stream or fountain? If so, you need access to an electricity supply. This could be in the house, or in a garage or shed that has mains power connected. Most pumps are supplied with 9m (30ft) of cable; solar

LEFT: *A small cascade adds movement to a secluded corner.*

power is a possibility for, say, a fountain further away from a source of electricity, though it is very expensive; or you could simply opt for a water feature that does not need a pump.

THE CORRECT SITE

It's important to choose the right site. For a pond you need a sheltered spot that gets at least six hours of sunlight each day and that is well away from deciduous trees, as fallen leaves will cause problems in autumn. In the shade few pond plants thrive: here a water feature like a fountain which does not have any plants or fish will be a much better choice, and water brightens up a dull area with reflected light and sparkle. It is always a good idea to put a water feature where you can see it from the house – and where you can get all round it easily, for maintenance later.

Lastly, the sort of feature you choose needs to suit its surroundings in scale and style. There is a huge range of formal and informal water features to suit virtually any type of house and garden.

ABOVE: *Covering a pond with a metal grid will make it safer for young children.*

charlie says . . .

If you're worried about the cost of building a water feature, or if you have a small garden, remember that they don't have to be grand or expensive. Calculate what you can afford to spend and plan your feature carefully. Container ponds, for example, are ideal for small gardens as they are fairly quick to install, take up little space and, if you keep things simple, are relatively inexpensive to maintain. You can experiment with all kinds of materials too, our driftwood fountain (left), is made out of attractive pieces of wood that look beautiful and give a really natural effect.

water garden maintenance

Fish and plants in a pond generate waste that forms sediment and feeds algae, which between them create a lot of work. Water-only features are much less effort, but pebble fountains where the water gets much less exposure to light and debris are the least labour-intensive.

WATER FEATURES (WITHOUT FISH OR PLANTS)

Spring Spring-clean if needed. Remove green pebbles, scrub clean and replace them. Alternatively use an algicide in the water: this won't totally stop algae growing, but it will slow them down.

Autumn If leaves get into the water feature, their decomposition creates nutrients that encourage algae, which clog the filter on your pump. Empty, scrub out and refill it. Small or raised water features, especially in containers, may need to be drained in winter to prevent them freezing solid. In this case take the pump out, dry and clean it and store it in a dry, frost-free place.

TOP: *Protect fish in winter by using a pond heater to keep a hole in the ice.*

RIGHT: *Divide overgrown plants in spring to encourage new growth and prevent plants becoming potbound.*

RIGHT: Iris versicolor: *a very attractive marginal iris with many dainty flowers.*

PONDS (WITH FISH AND/OR PLANTS)

Early spring Start feeding fish, but only lightly. If oxygenating plants have been killed off in winter, add more now.

Spring Every five to seven years divide overgrown marginal plants and water lilies once they are in active growth. (But leave irises until just after flowering, so you don't miss a season's blooms.) You can add new water plants to the pond any time from mid-spring to late summer. Buy those growing in planting baskets, or plant loose plants in net pots using special pond-plant soil, then cover the surface with 2.5cm (1in) of gravel and put them straight in the pond. Sit deep-water aquatics, water lilies and oxygenators on the base of the pond and marginals on a planting shelf so that the crown is covered by the right depth of water.

Important: the depth given on the planting label of a water plant refers to the depth of water above the crown of the plant not the depth of the planting shelf you stand it on.

Summer Thin out overgrown oxygenators and/or lily leaves as it becomes necessary.

Autumn Reduce fish feeding. Cut plants back to the top of their baskets when they start to die back after the first hard frost. Using a fine net, scoop out some of the sediment that builds up in the bottom of a mature pond, but leave 2.5–5cm (1–2in) behind.

Winter Keep a hole in the ice so that fish can get oxygen and are not poisoned by carbon dioxide. The best way to do this is to substitute a pond heater for the pump.

THE MAJOR OVERHAUL

More drastic maintenance is needed about every five to seven years, when there is 15–18cm (6–7in) of sediment in the bottom of the pond. The time to do this is late spring. First take out all the plants. There is no need to remove all the water, so you may not need to catch the fish. In fact it's best not to empty the pond as the water is mature – if you refill it with 'new' tap water, this can bring in nutrients that unbalance the microscopic life of the pond. Clear out a lot of the sediment. Don't try to make the pond completely clean, but leave some sediment on the bottom. Divide and repot plants that need it, top up the pond and replace them.

the technical side

At its simplest you don't need much to start water gardening. But if you want fountains, waterfalls, streams or lighting, you need electricity, a pump and perhaps other gadgets too. People are always – rightly – concerned about safety where water and electricity are concerned, so if you are unhappy about installing it yourself, get an electrician to do it for you.

THE ELECTRICITY SUPPLY

Pond pumps come with 9m (30ft) of cable. This needs to be run through a conduit pipe (for instance, reinforced hosepipe) to protect it from harm. The way we do it on *Ground Force* is to thread a string tied to a heavy nail at one end through the conduit pipe, shake it down the tube, and use the string to pull the power cable through. Then bury the conduit pipe in the garden, or under paving or decking to hide it. Drill a hole through the house wall, feed the electric cable through the wall and connect it to a three-pin plug on the other side. Plug into a normal socket fitted with a circuit breaker: this cuts the power immediately in case of problems, so there is no risk of getting a shock. Use a low-voltage pump as a 'belt and braces' measure. Alternatively get an electrician to put in armoured cable and a weatherproof outdoor box with the cables wired permanently in.

LEFT: *When deciding on the position of your water feature, think about how much maintenance you will need to do and plan accordingly. Fountains, for example, need to be installed where they can be easily reached as the nozzle will get clogged and you need to be able to clear it without having to clamber over the rest of the garden. Poke out the debris using a straightened paperclip, or pull off the rose and wash it under the tap. If you use the paperclip method, leave the jet turned on and you'll see the jet playing more freely as you get rid of the build-up. To keep clogging down to a minimum, you can get pumps with a pre-filter that will sieve out a lot of the debris.*

POND PUMPS

We always use submersible pumps on *Ground Force*. These are suitable for all but really big water gardening projects. The pump always goes at the lowest point of the system, but don't sit it on the bottom of the pond, particularly if you are including fish or plants, or it will suck in sediment which can clog it up. Stand it 7.5–10cm (3–4in) off the base on an upturned pond basket. Small pumps will need fixing in place.

Pump prices range from £25 to £100s. Don't assume the cheapest will do – it must be big enough for the job. Take advice. The maker's leaflet tells you the output of the pump in gallons per hour. This determines the height the pump can push the water (measure the drop between the top of a waterfall or fountain and the water outlet) and the size and type of fountain the pump can run. A rose spray fountain, for instance, does not need a big pump, but a bell fountain needs one that can cope with about 1820–2730 litres (400–600 gallons) per hour.

ABOVE: *Constructing the lion's head fountain (see page 72).*
The water pipes are cleverly concealed using second-hand pantiles.

ABOVE: *Installing the fountain in the hexagonal pond (see page 52).*
This pond is an ideal beginner's project as the pieces simply slot together.

Low-voltage pumps are ideal for people worried about using electricity in a pond; they are suitable for small schemes but are capable of pumping only up to about 2950 litres (650 gallons) per hour. Solar-powered pumps are in their early stages yet, cost about four and a half times as much as equivalent electric pumps, and the power drops in dull weather. But they are ideal for people who don't like the idea of using electricity in water, who are environmentally aware, or whose pond is a long way from a power point.

Pump Care

In winter, if you leave the pump in the pond, run it every few weeks to keep the bearings and the impeller free. If you take the pump out, clean it, dry it and store it indoors where it stays dry, or it will seize up.

In summer, clean the filter on the front of the pump (if it has one) every week otherwise it can get clogged with sediment or algae that restrict the water going through it and can damage it. The longer you run your pump, the more likely it is to get blocked up. Clean fountain nozzles too as they also become blocked.

lining
a pond

Ponds need lining to allow them to hold water. Don't rely on puddled clay soil – it rarely works – and concrete is slow to use and expensive. Nowadays we mostly use flexible liners made of thin sheets of plastic or rubbery fabric, or preformed pond 'shells' made of fibreglass. Although preformed shells may at first look like the easier option, they are trickier to put in than flexible liners and cost more to buy. The range of shapes and sizes available is limited too. A flexible liner allows you to make a pond any shape you like, and any size from a puddle to a full-grown lake. If you are making a complicated water garden, it pays to buy the best butyl liner: this way you won't have to redo it in a hurry.

ABOVE: *Wooden poles form a modern surround to this pond.*
BELOW: *Raised pond edges can be used for extra seating.*

ABOVE: *Always mark out the shape of a pond before starting to dig.*

WHAT LINER?

Flexible liners
Black polythene Many garden uses, but not tough enough for pond liner or even for lining a bog garden. Life expectancy: two to three years.

PVC The cheapest type of liner, this goes brittle in sunlight, so expect your pond to crack round the rim where it is not covered by water. Unlike small punctures inside the pond, cracks round the rim cannot be satisfactorily repaired. PVC is fine for a short-term project or where it is easily replaced, but best for lining a bog garden, where it is buried in the soil safe from sunlight. Life expectancy: five to ten years.

Long-life PVC This is a superior type of PVC liner which has been treated with a chemical to keep it supple for longer, so it won't crack in sunlight. This is naturally more expensive, but much longer-lasting. Some long-life PVCs are reinforced with nylon, which makes them stronger but may not prevent them becoming brittle. Life expectancy: up to twenty-five years.

Butyl rubber Thin, supple and stretchy, this is the best type of lining material as it 'gives' slightly if the soil should settle in years to come. Butyl is long-lasting, provided it is not holed by animal claws or someone stepping into the pond carelessly when cleaning it. Life expectancy: twenty-five years plus.

Rigid liners
'Shell' liners These are available in two grades, but both take more time and trouble to install than a PVC or butyl liner. The semi-rigid are cheaper, but won't last as long as the rigid sort, and as the sides are rather floppy they are tricky to put in because they move about all the time. Life expectancy: five to ten years. The truly rigid shapes cost more, but will last for at least twenty-five years if installed well.

WORKING OUT HOW MUCH FLEXIBLE LINER TO BUY
Measure up or calculate the length and breadth of your pond, then add twice the maximum depth of the pond to both measurements. In the case of an odd-shaped informal pond, imagine the shape fitted into an oblong and measure the length and breadth of that, then add twice the maximum depth to each.

THE PROJECTS

CONTAINER PONDS

Container ponds are one of the fastest-growing areas of water gardening, as they look wonderful and are quick, easy and inexpensive to set up. They are ideal for people on the move because you don't need to do any construction, and they can easily be packed up and taken with you. They are naturally compact, perfect for very tiny gardens and also very child-friendly.

FAR LEFT: *For a small garden, miniature pools like this tiny lily pool, take up very little space and look beautiful.*

LEFT: *The New Zealand tree fern in the centre of this stone pool will make attractive reflections in the water surrounding it.*

RIGHT: *Half-barrels make perfect container ponds and are relatively easy to construct and maintain.*

Almost anything that holds water can be used as a container pond, so there is plenty of creative potential. At its simplest it can be just a small fountain in a bowl. Or you could have a potted pond complete with fish, miniature water lily, marginal plants and oxygenators. A clear glass bowl containing a handful of floating tropical water plants, like water lettuce or water hyacinth, makes a fascinating table-top feature for a conservatory too. Because the temperature can fluctuate a lot in a small container, put a miniature pond like this in a sheltered corner where it won't be in hot sun all day long.

WINTER CARE

In winter move the complete container pond under cover if you can, as many kinds of container will crack when the water in them freezes and expands. A greenhouse, carport or porch is fine. Otherwise drain it during the coldest months. If you leave even an empty ceramic or terracotta container outside, turn it upside down to stop it filling with rainwater, again to avoid cracking.

What to Use

✔ *Choose large ceramic or plastic plant containers, deep birdbaths, half-barrels and decorative containers of all sorts.*

✘ *Avoid plastic containers as they become brittle in sunlight. Also avoid metal that rusts – it leaches toxins into the water.*

If you buy a terracotta or ceramic container without a hole in the base, use a sharp masonry bit to drill one. To avoid cracking the pot, use a small drill and make three small holes close together, then join them up to make one larger one with a file or rasp, or use progressively larger drill bits. If you are nervous about trying it, look out for suitable containers that have already been drilled as they are often available.

Galvanized containers are safe to use if you first paint them with black bitumastic paint to seal in the zinc: essential if you want to add fish and plants. Check that paints are fish-friendly – buy them at a specialist water garden centre.

round stone pond

This is a very easy project as there is no moving water, so there are no electrics or pipes to bother with. It makes an ideal 'first pond' for anyone who has never tried water gardening before and is sure to lead you on to greater things. It is an extremely versatile go-anywhere sort of feature that would look good in the middle of a tiny formal garden, but would also suit a contemporary type of garden. It would not be out of place in a Mediterranean-style or gravel garden, standing among cobblestones, on a patio or in a border surrounded by low plants. You could even get away with it in a pocket-sized wildlife garden as an alternative to a sunken pool. As there are no water plants, use an algicide to stop the water turning green and slime building up on the inside of the container.

TIME
Two hours, but allow four hours for sealant to dry.

CHILD FRIENDLY
Fairly.

MAINTENANCE
Low.

COST
About £200.

YOU WILL NEED
- Concrete container about 90cm (3ft) in diameter and 30cm (1ft) deep
- Liquid resin sealant
- Pebbles and different-sized smooth stones
- Pot (to match that of the dicksonia)
- *Dicksonia antarctica*: 1 in pot
- Phormium: 1
- *Phyllostachys aurea*: 1

1 Choose a suitable container and just stand it in position on level ground. The one we used on the *Ground Force* programme was a large, porous, concrete bowl originally intended for plants, so it had a hole in the bottom that we had to stop up first. To waterproof it I painted the inside with liquid resin and left it to dry thoroughly.

2 Put a few handfuls of pebbles in the base of the container to make the interior look more interesting, then fill it with water.

3 Stand a plinth in the middle with a potted plant on top (you could use an upturned clay flowerpot, with a matching one on top to create a 'column'). We used a *Dicksonia antarctica* (New Zealand tree fern), whose foliage forms a fountain shape and makes wonderful reflections. But any moisture-loving plant with architectural foliage looks good.

4 Plant the surrounding soil with a large phormium and *Phyllostachys aurea* (variegated bamboo). When you are planting in soil that will later be mulched with pebbles, as in this case, leave the rootballs 2.5cm (1in) proud of the soil so that the pebbles don't bury the stems too deeply.

5 Cover the soil with different-sized smooth stones to suggest a dry stream bed. Alan used a mixture of cobblestones and 20–30mm- (about 1in-) sized Caledonian river pebbles; they look like sugared almonds when they are dry and colour up more when wet.

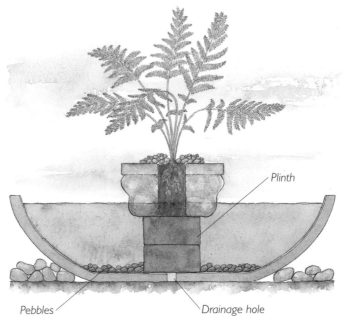

Plinth

Pebbles

Drainage hole sealed with silicon

barrel
pond

A barrel makes a very good, natural-looking container pond that associates brilliantly with water plants. You can use one on its own, or stand, say, three different-sized barrels close together in a corner of the patio, each filled with a different group of plants, to make a bigger feature. To make the most of the natural wood effect, try standing a barrel pond on bricks or tiles among shrubs in a woodland-style border; it would look great teamed with a smaller barrel planted with bog garden plants (see page 43). You can get half-barrels up to 1m (3ft) across, but 45cm (1½ft) diameter is a good size for a container pond as it is more movable.

TIME
Under one hour.

CHILD FRIENDLY
Yes.

MAINTENANCE
Medium.

COST
About £70.

YOU WILL NEED
- Half-barrel 45cm (1½ft) in diameter
- Miniature water lily: 1
- Oxygenating plants: 2
- Marginal plants: 3
- Goldfish: 2

WINTER CARE

A barrel is quite well insulated by its wooden sides, so in a very sheltered spot you could leave it standing outside during the winter. Unlike a ceramic container, it won't crack if the water freezes, though this won't do the inhabitants much good. If you don't have anywhere under cover to keep it during the coldest weather, dismantle the pond for the winter. Put the fish back into a pond or into a fish tank indoors. Protect the miniature water lily (they are expensive!) by lifting it out of the pond when it is dormant and potting it in a bowl of damp soil with a few centimetres of water over the top. Keep it in a conservatory, greenhouse or porch where it gets plenty of light but stays reasonably cold – water lilies need a winter rest, and won't like being kept indoors in winter.

1 Choose a suitable half-barrel 45cm (1½ft) in diameter and simply stand it in position on level ground. Fill with water.

2 Put in the plants in pond pots. For a barrel this size use one miniature water lily, two oxygenators and three marginal plants. Choose more compact marginals such as *Calla palustris* (bog arum) and *Sagittaria japonica* 'Plena'. For oxygenators use starwort or water violet. Stand the marginal plants on upturned pots so that their roots are covered by the right depth of water.

3 After two weeks, when everything has settled down, add two small, colourful goldfish, following the same technique as when introducing fish into a normal pond (see page 89).

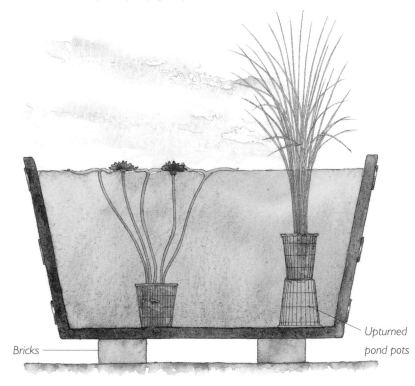

Bricks

Upturned pond pots

natural driftwood fountain

This is a more sophisticated version of a container pond, using a pretty, blue ceramic jar and a small fountain. It would look absolutely stunning on a patio or in a conservatory, or in a courtyard garden. It also makes a good centrepiece for a tiny formal garden, especially teamed with a mosaic that echoes the blue of the container. The jar is in fact a plant pot with a drainage hole in the bottom, through which I passed the electric cable for the pump. You need only a tiny pump to go in a jar like this. The one I used is the size of a clenched fist, and pumps 28 litres (6 gallons) an hour, enough to create a small ripple, which is all you want in a container this size. (If you used a bigger fountain, the water would run out over the sides of the jar and soon empty it.) If you want to follow our design exactly, you will need driftwood to stick around the water outlet – most florists or water garden centres will stock it. Join the pieces together with silicon to achieve the effect you want.

TIME
About one hour, but allow twenty-four hours for sealant to dry.

CHILD FRIENDLY
Yes.

MAINTENANCE
Low.

COST
About £120.

YOU WILL NEED
- Glazed ceramic plant pot about 30cm (1ft) in diameter and 45cm (1½ft) deep
- Small submersible pump with cable
- Conduit for cable
- Circuit breaker
- Planting baskets: 2
- Gravel and pebbles
- driftwood (from a florist or garden centre)
- Silicon sealant
- Grasses
- Bamboos

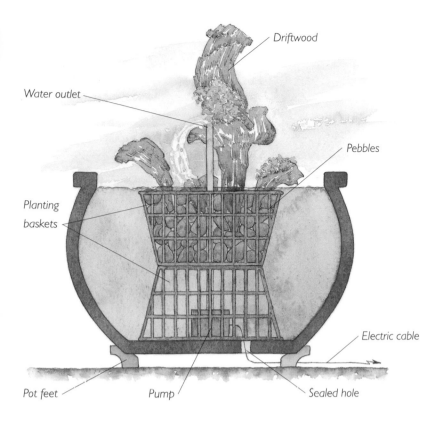

Driftwood

Water outlet

Pebbles

Planting baskets

Electric cable

Pot feet

Pump

Sealed hole

ABOVE: We used driftwood in our container, but you could experiment with other materials.

1 Choose a level site for the pot and dig a narrow channel for the electric cable, which comes out through the central hole in the bottom. The cable must not kink or make the pot lean over to one side. Alternatively, raise the container up on pot feet so the cable can come out underneath without any obstructions.

2 Run the cable through a conduit in a trench, so that it won't be damaged by human traffic or digging, and drill a hole through the house wall to take it to a power point where it can be plugged in via an earth leakage circuit breaker for safety.

3 Make a level bed of gravel for the pot and stand it in position.

4 Put the pump inside the pot and thread the electric cable through the hole in the pot base. The pump must sit bolt upright to ensure that the ripples from the fountain come out evenly all round, not all over to one side. Then use a tube of silicon to seal up the hole all round the cable, making a watertight join. Smear the rest of the silicon over the base of the pot to waterproof it too.

5 Place two planting baskets base-to-base over the top of the pump, pushing the water outlet through the holes in the bottom of the baskets. Fill the top basket with coloured stones and pebbles and stick attractive pieces of driftwood around the water outlet using clear silicon.

6 Fill the pot with water. Turn on the pump and adjust the flow so that the water trickles gently over the wood.

7 Since the fountain creates too much water turbulence for fish or plants to thrive, surround the pool with pebbles and 'watery-themed' plants such as grasses and bamboos instead.

charlie says...

You can make all sorts of fountain surrounds or things to hide pipework with clear silicon. Use it to stick pebbles together, to glue copper to glass, or wood to rock so long as both objects are clean and dry. Choose a zinc-free brand for ponds containing plants or fish.

SUNKEN PONDS WITH LINERS

Flexible pond liners are quick and easy to install and, depending which sort you use, relatively cheap to buy. They are terrifically versatile. You can make a formal pond with straight edges and vertical sides, or a natural-looking pond with a curvy, informal shape.

ABOVE: *For a naturalistic pond, conceal the liner with native plants.*

RIGHT: *Paving slabs are a more formal way of hiding a pond liner.*

TOP: *Flexible liners are very versatile and can be used as the basis for dramatic water features.*

You can make 'stepped' planting shelves to stand pots of marginal plants on, or have gently shelving sides which are ideal for wildlife ponds as they let birds bathe and hedgehogs or froglets get in and out. You can also use pond liner to make creative waterfalls or bog gardens. Best of all, using flexible pond liner, you can make your pond whatever shape or size you like. Sheets of butyl can even be 'welded' together on site to line a whole lake. But some people prefer the 'easy' option of choosing a ready-made pond shape moulded from fibreglass. With these you are restricted in the sizes and shapes available, and they don't save you any digging – in fact, I think they are harder to put in than a pond with a flexible liner. But they let you see in advance what you are going to get, which makes planning easier. They also save all that fussing around trying to get a sheet of liner to sit in the hole and then smoothing out the creases so you don't have big, thick folds of spare material in the corners. And some people just prefer them.

HIDING THE EDGES

One thing I hate to see is a pond where the liner is showing all round the edge. Whether a fibreglass or flexible liner is used, the edge should be out of sight. The way most people achieve this is by laying paving to make a firm surface round the pond, which gives you both a safe place to stand and hides the edge of the liner permanently. To lay the slabs dig a 'groove' around the pond just behind the edge of the liner. Lay a bed of mortar about 2.5cm (1in) deep with a trowel, bringing it level with the lip of the pond. (To make this, mix 2 parts sharp sand, 2 parts soft sand and 1 part cement, or buy ready-mixed bags of 4 in 1, and mix to a sloppy goo with water. Don't use the mixture dry as it gets in the water and harms pondlife.) Then, while this is wet, lay the slabs on to it so that

they overhang the edge of the pond slightly. Fill the gaps between them with gravel or mortar.

The alternative is to surround the pond with plants. Use creeping Jenny, water forget-me-not and veronica, which grow half-in and half-out of the water. Or make a bog garden round the pond and let bog plants hide the join. But if the soil is very dry, grow creeping thymes and other rock plants, plus horizontal dwarf junipers. It's important to use evergreens, otherwise you'll still see the liner in winter when herbaceous waterside and bog plants die back.

formal water lily pond

A circular hole is the very easiest shape to fit a flexible liner into, so this type of pond is a good project for a novice water gardener to start with. Other regular geometric shapes such as rectangles and squares are also reasonably easy. You don't have to have a totally formal garden for this type of pond to look good, though formal surroundings – paving and symmetrical geometric-shaped beds – do show it off best. It would make an attractive centrepiece for a small enclosed garden, or a small formal 'garden room' like the one Alan created for the *Ground Force* programme: it gave a great view from the summerhouse!

Obviously you can copy the techniques used in this project to make a pond of any size you like. Just follow the steps overleaf, remembering to adjust the size of the liner accordingly (see page 17 for how to calculate the amount of liner you will need).

TIME
Two days (digging and lining pond, one day; paving, one day).

CHILD FRIENDLY
No.

MAINTENANCE
High.

COST
About £280.

YOU WILL NEED
For a pond 2.1m (7ft) in diameter and 45cm (1¹/₂ft) deep with 23cm– (9in-)deep shelf all round
- Butyl liner 3 × 3m (10 × 10ft)
- Damp soft builder's sand
- Paving slabs and cement mix
- *Elodea canadensis*: 4 bunches in planting baskets of pond soil
- *Elodea crispa*: 6 bunches in planting baskets of pond soil
- *Iris laevigata*: 6
- *Myriophyllum spicatum*: 4 in planting baskets
- Water lily: 2 small or medium-sized

1 Mark out a circle (see tip opposite) and dig a hole 23cm (9in) deep then mark out a central 'pit' and dig to 46cm (18in) deep. Line the entire shape with 5cm (2in) of damp soft sand – use a plasterer's float to smooth the sand down.

2 Open out the liner and, with someone at each end, lift it over the prepared hole. Lower it gently down and let it 'relax' into the depression.

3 You'll need to get into the pond at this stage to help the material fit perfectly into the shape, so take your shoes off to avoid tearing the liner. Ease the material into 'pleats' round the planting shelf and even out the creases so that they are distributed all round the shape.

4 Start to fill the pond with water, leaving the hose running slowly: the weight of the water will help the liner to cling neatly into the shape. Continue to ease out wrinkles so they don't all end up in great folds.

5 Don't trim the edge of the liner until the pond is full of water, as the material always sinks down. Tidy the edges, by cutting the liner, leaving about 15–30cm (6–12in) of overlap all round the sides. Then hide the edge by laying paving (see page 29). Finally, sit the plants in position, making sure that their roots are covered by the correct depth of water.

Paving slabs cover liner edge

Butyl liner

Sand

Planting shelf

TRICKS OF THE TRADE: GET IT LEVEL

When you are making a lined pond, you must keep the rim level. If one part of the pond ends up lower than the rest, the water will run out at that point, leaving huge expanses of liner showing all round the rest of the pond, which you won't be able to hide. I like to level the site roughly by eye before even starting to dig the hole. Use a spade to scrape soil off the bumps and into the hollows. Then check it with a spirit level in both directions – lengthways and crossways. Use a long spirit level resting on a suitable straight edge: a 1.8m (6ft) plank is ideal. Once you are certain that the ground is level, you are ready to dig the pond. When you have finished, get rid of the spoil and leave a clear 30–45cm- (1–1 $\frac{1}{2}$ft-)wide strip all round the edge of the hole. Check the level again, adding or removing soil as needed. The beauty of a flexible pond liner is that it is still possible to tuck a little extra soil under the edge or remove any surplus even after the liner is in place and the pond is filled with water. This is why I would recommend a flexible liner if you are making your first pond, as it is much more difficult to adjust a fibreglass shell once it's in place.

TO AVOID LEAKS LATER

After digging the hole for the pond, pick out any visible stones or large roots from the sides. These could easily perforate a butyl or PVC liner once the weight of the water presses it down. But it is also advisable to 'cushion' the liner more, so spread a 5cm (2in) layer of sand in the bottom. I pinch Tommy's soft builder's sand. (Avoid the coarse, gritty kind as the sharp particles are enough to make a leak.) Use damp sand as it sticks to the sides of the hole better. Where ground is very stony, use special pond underlay (ask for bonded fibre) as this stops flints and roots getting through, but put a layer of sand on top of this too. Use the bonded fibre on its own in places where you cannot 'plaster' the inside of a pond shape with sand: for instance, vertical brick walls surrounding a formal pond (bricks have sharp edges!). Then lower the liner into place. You could use old carpet underlay instead, and the reason we don't use it on *Ground Force* is simply that it is quicker and easier for us to pick up proper underlay when we buy the rest of our purchases. We are always trying to beat the clock!

pond with rockery

This water garden, based round a rockery with a two-spouted waterfall, is one of the most complex we have ever done on *Ground Force*. If you fancy something similar at home, do it in easy stages, and get some hefty helpers: shifting big boulders is back-breaking work! Careful planning is essential – work out where your electricity supply will be before you start. You should definitely use a butyl liner for this project, so you won't need to replace it for twenty to twenty-five years: it will be a major job. See page 17 for how to calculate the size you need to buy, and get enough extra to extend beyond the far end of the pool and up the full height of the rockery, to make the cascade of the waterfall.

TIME
Four days or more.

CHILD FRIENDLY
No.

MAINTENANCE
Medium.

COST
About £1860.

YOU WILL NEED

For a pond 2.4 × 1.2m × 46cm deep (8 × 4ft × 18in deep) and rockery 4.6 × 6.1m (15 × 20ft)

- Butyl liner for the pond 3.3 × 2.1m (11 × 7ft)
- Butyl liner for the cascade 2.1 × 1.5m (7 × 5ft)
- Damp soft builder's sand
- Paving slabs and cement mix
- Rocks and stone chippings
- Submersible pump (1200 gallons per hour)
- Conduit for cable and circuit breaker
- Hosepipe 2.5cm (1in) in diameter
- T-piece
- *Acer palmatum cultivar*: 1
- *Caltha palustris* 'Flore Pleno': 1
- *Carex elata* 'Aurea': 1
- *Ranunculus acris* 'Flore Pleno': 1
- Suitable rockery plants (see overleaf)

You could create a feature like this in virtually any garden, in town or country, where there is room – it takes up a lot more space than a pond on its own. It does need a very natural-looking garden around it. I'd suggest banks of shrubs with winding gravel paths and lawns, perhaps even a small wildflower area, for the rest of the garden – like the one in the television programme which was created to remind the owner of her Yorkshire roots. Shrubs or wildflowers would also be low-maintenance, allowing you to spend more time looking after the rock garden which always takes quite a bit of regular work.

Of course, you don't have to make such a large feature as the one described here. If your garden and/or ambitions are more modest, you can use the same techniques on a smaller scale, with excellent results. The added bonus is that you won't need so much liner or so many rocks, so the feature will be a lot cheaper to construct.

BELOW: A rockery like this one does look dramatic and is worth the extra trouble that it takes to construct. Plan the layout carefully before you set to work as once everything is in position it will be a major job to move it.

THE POND PLANTING

Round the edge of the pond is a planting shelf 23cm (9in) deep, on which stand pots of *Carex elata* 'Aurea' (Bowles golden sedge), *Caltha palustris* 'Flore Pleno' and *Ranunculus acris* 'Flore Pleno'. Avoid putting plants directly under the waterfall as they won't survive and steer clear of water lilies as there is too much splashing water for them to be happy.

THE ROCKERY PLANTING

Fill the gaps between the rocks with topsoil to make free-draining planting pockets for alpines. Group the plants in threes or fives to give a mature look fast. Use small, compact and carpeting plants like *Raoulia australis* (vegetable sheep), *Androsace sarmentosa*, dwarf conifers, *Viola* 'Bowles Black', *Armeria maritima* and potentillas. If you want a good shrub for the top of the rockery, plant an *Acer palmatum cultivar* (Japanese maple) as we did. After planting, spread a 2.5cm (1in) layer of stone chippings all over the rockery to stop the plants getting splashed with mud or rotting at the collar; it also suppresses weeds.

Rocks

✔ *Do use local stone if possible as it looks more natural.*

✘ *Don't use water-worn limestone ripped up from the countryside. Reuse old stone from a Victorian rockery, or choose hollow synthetic rock, or reconstituted stone. You'll find the biggest choice at a stone merchant.*

✔ *Do choose gravel in a matching colour for a natural effect.*

✔ *Do get rocks delivered close to the site to avoid having to move them more than necessary. Use levers like big crowbars to ease them into position.*

✔ *Do arrange rocks so that they look like natural strata and are not just dotted about on a mound of earth.*

✘ *Don't try to bury rocks two-thirds in the ground as Victorian rockery builders insisted. They are expensive and you want to see as much of them as you can!*

1 Make the main pond as described on page 32 and pave round the edges as on page 29.

2 Place the submersible pump in the deepest part of the pond and attach the cable to the electricity supply as described on page 27. We dug a trench for the power cable, running from the pond under the patio (we had to lift a few slabs) and, via a hole through the wall, into the conservatory. We ran the cable through a conduit, so that it won't be damaged by any future digging.

3 Create the shape of the rockery by mounding up topsoil. Make terraces of rock on this, using stones in proportion to the size of the rockery. To make the rocks secure, bed them on to a well-compacted surface. We used a pickaxe handle to ram the soil down. Where the rocks run down into the pond, stand them on 'mats' cut from offcuts of the pond liner, to protect the liner from sharp edges. For the project shown in the *Ground Force* programme, we had to make a retaining wall along one side of the

rock garden to stop the soil piling up against the neighbour's fence. This was done by cutting two long concrete fence posts in half, burying the bottom 60cm (2ft) in the ground, then slotting concrete panels into them to hold back the soil. Obviously most projects won't require such measures.

4 Build the soil up at the back of the rockery to form the waterfall feature. To make the cascade, line the slope of the rockery with a separate piece of butyl, leaving the end overhanging the pond (that way, all the water runs back into the pond). Then make an upright rock-face by rendering the liner with a strong cement mix (3 parts sand to 1 part cement) and, while it is wet, pushing in rocks to create as natural a look as possible. This not only hides the black butyl, but also makes the water splash and sparkle as it runs down. If the rocks don't quite meet together in front of the liner, mortar the gaps and push some stone chippings into the cracks.

5 Make a mini pond at the top of the rockery to act as a 'header pond' into which water is recycled via the pump in the main pond, to form the waterfall. This must be lined slightly above the normal water level, since the water splashes up when it runs out of the pipe from the pump. (If it runs out over the edge of the header pond, your pond will eventually run dry.) Connect a length of 2.5cm- (1in-)diameter hosepipe to the pump and run it to the outlet at the top of the waterfall, hiding it in the rockwork along the side of the pond and up the back of the water feature. To make a two-spouted fountain like the one we showed in the *Ground Force* programme, fit a T-piece to the end of the hosepipe, from which two pipes supply water to two different places in the rockwork. Make one outlet bigger than the other for a more natural look.

6 Add the plants to the main pond and plant up the rockery.

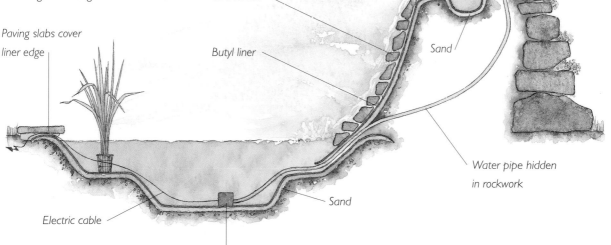

Paving slabs cover liner edge

Cascade made of cement and stones

Butyl liner

Header pond

Water outlet

Sand

Water pipe hidden in rockwork

Electric cable

Sand

Pump

wildlife
pond

A wildlife pond needs a very natural type of garden around it, but you don't have to live in the country – it would not look out of place in an estate garden or in town. It is a wonderful way to encourage a huge range of birds, insects, small mammals, amphibians and even reptiles to visit your garden. It also gives you a perfect environment for landscaping with wild flowers. The difference between this type of pond and more formal kinds is that a wildlife pond is easier to make and maintain.

TIME
Two days.

CHILD FRIENDLY
Fairly.

MAINTENANCE
Low.

COST
About £200.

YOU WILL NEED
For a pond 1.8 × 1.5m × 60cm deep
(6 × 5 × 2ft deep)
- Butyl liner 3 × 2.4m (10 × 8ft)
- Boards and aquatic soil
- Bonded fibre underlay
- Damp soft builder's sand
- Large and small stones/gravel
- Suitable plants (see page 41)

It has gently shelving sides all round so that creatures can get in and out easily and use it for drinking and bathing. And there are no planting pockets; this is the only sort of pond where I'd suggest planting straight into a muddy bottom. Because your plants will be bare-rooted (not growing in pond baskets), they will cost less. Use native plants, but be careful which you choose as some can be very vigorous. Hide the edge of the liner with plants and smooth stones for a natural effect, and perhaps flank the pond with fallen logs or a tree stump. Or simply extend the liner outwards all round the pond to make a surrounding bog garden (see page 42) – with a wildlife pool there is no need to keep the two separate, as you normally should.

ABOVE: *The gently shelving sides of the pool give visiting wildlife easy access to the water.*

RIGHT: *Native plants conceal the pond liner and make the pond look more established.*

Gravel and large stones

Boards retain soil
and pebbles

Sand

Aquatic soil

Bonded fibre

Butyl liner

Bonded fibre

1 Dig a dish-shaped depression with gently sloping sides, going down to about 45–60cm (1½–2ft) deep in the middle. Spread a 2.5–5cm (1–2in) layer of damp soft sand all over this, then lay a butyl liner over the top (see page 32). If you want plants, prepare a special area for them before putting the liner in position. Surround the planting place with boards laid on edge and lay the liner over this so you have a depression to retain the soil.

2 Lay bonded fibre (which is normally used as a pond underlay) over that part of the liner where you are going to plant and cover this with soil. This helps to keep the soil where you want it. Use special aquatic soil or plain clay-loam from part of the garden where no fertilizers or chemicals have been used.

3 Fill the pond with water (see page 32).

4 Plant straight into the soil on the bottom of the pond, starting with deep-water aquatics near the middle; put shallower marginals where they will grow in about 15–23cm (6–9in) of water, and bog plants round the edges. Use these to hide the edge of your liner in places, and run a mixture of large and small stones or gravel down into the water elsewhere. There is no need to cover the floor of the pond with stones.

charlie says . . .

Don't introduce wildlife, even frogspawn. Let it find you. If nothing much arrives, it means that your wildlife pond is not yet ready for it. Encourage wildlife by not cleaning up too much or splitting plants too soon. Pile up rotting logs to encourage grubs and insects and to provide a place for hedgehogs to hibernate, and leave the area undisturbed. Plant marginals with upright stems, like iris and butomus, so that dragonfly nymphs can pull themselves up out of the water when they are changing into adults. Don't put fish in a wildlife pond, unless you can get sticklebacks. They are fine because they are natives.

ABOVE AND LEFT: *Birds and frogs are likely to be regular visitors to your pond, while dragonflies* (RIGHT) *are a more unusual sight.*

UNDESIRABLE WILDLIFE

Ducks These are unwelcome. It sounds mean, but chase them off. (They are most likely to visit in spring when they are looking for nesting places.) Ducks pull up your plants, eat them and make a lot of waste which turns water green and smelly. They wreck your liner by scrambling up it, as they use the same place to get in and out all the time. And they make a dreadful mess of your grass. Your pretty bog garden will become a real bog. If you must have ornamental ducks, fence off a separate pond for them, made of concrete so you can scrub it clean regularly.

Midges There is no need to introduce fish to eat midge and mosquito larvae. Newts and dragonfly larvae will feed on them too. But my favourite solution, for a wildlife pond, is to grow insectivorous plants like sundew, butterwort and sarracenia (huntsman's cup) in the boggy margins around it. They look stunning, grown among bits of gnarled wood, and they really do work. Leave them in their pots and plunge them in place for the summer – they need winter protection in a cool greenhouse.

Recommended Plants

Native plants look most natural, but choose only compact, well-behaved kinds such as the following:

Alisma plantago-aquatica *(water plantain)*
Rosettes of green, lance-shaped leaves, with airy, 60cm (2ft) sprays of tiny, pale pink flowers in late summer.

Caltha palustris *(kingcup)*
The single, yellow sort that self-seeds gently and grows in shallow water and boggy margins. Chop back hard when it gets untidy.

Butomus umbellatus *(flowering rush)*
A tall, stately plant with upright, rush-like stems topped by pink, cartwheel-shaped flowers in mid- to late summer. It grows best in 25cm (10in) of water.

Menyanthes trifoliata *(bog bean)*
This grows in shallow water and spreads out nicely over the water surface. Good 'broad bean' foliage and frilly, white, late spring flowers.

Lythrum salicaria *(purple loosestrife)*
Tall, rosy-purple spikes of flowers in late summer; grow in boggy pond surrounds or on the marginal shelf with 7.5–10cm (3–4in) of water above. Pinch out the tops in early spring to make shorter and bushier.

Sagittaria japonica *(arrowhead)*
Big, tall, stunning, arrowhead-shaped leaves, plus spikes of white flowers in mid- to late summer, for water about 15cm (6in) deep.

bog
garden

⏱ **TIME**

One day.

🎲 **CHILD FRIENDLY**

Pond: no. Bog garden: yes.

✋ **MAINTENANCE**

Pond: high. Bog garden: low.

💰 **COST**

About £50 (not including the cost of the pond).

💧 **YOU WILL NEED**

For a pond (size of your choice) and adjoining bog garden 1.8 × 1.2m (6 × 4ft)

- Butyl liner for the pond (see page 17 for how to calculate size)
- PVC liner for the bog garden 2.1 × 1.5m (7 × 5ft)
- Boards and pond compost for the pond
- Bonded fibre underlay for the pond
- Large stones, small stones/gravel
- Damp soft builder's sand
- Suitable bog plants (see opposite)
- Suitable pond plants (see pages 82-7)

charlie says . . .

Since bog and pond plants all die down in winter, add a gnarled tree stump, a pile of mossy logs or some red-stemmed cornus shrubs for architectural interest.

Ponds and bog gardens are natural partners. Water doubles the value of plants growing alongside it by reflecting them, while bog plants have such dramatic leaves and spectacular flowers you would think they were deliberately designed to be seen from both sides at once. I like to make a bog garden with an informal or natural style of pond, or alongside a semi-formal feature like a pebble pool. There is no need to make the bog garden run right round the water – you could have a deep bog garden at the back to grow tall plants, and a shallow bog at the front for primulas and hostas. You can even grow bog plants in a container without any drainage holes on the patio, to give the right sort of background planting to a container pond.

Where people often go wrong is by making ponds and bogs so that water can run from one into the other. This is a recipe for disaster. When soil gets into a pond, it brings nutrients that turn the water green or choke it with blanket weed. Keep the pond and bog garden close, but separate. Bog gardens fail if they dry out in summer and maintenance is very difficult if they get totally waterlogged. The method I use avoids all these problems.

You can make the pond and adjoining bog garden as described here, or just the bog garden on its own, and you can, of course, adapt the size of each to suit your particular site and preferences.

Recommended Bog Garden Plants

Gunnera manicata
Stunning, 1.8 × 1.8m (6 × 6ft) giant producing amazing reflections in water. Cover the crown with a 'tent' of its own dead leaves in winter, adding extra straw for young plants.

Darmera peltata
Pink flowers push up from bare soil in spring, followed later by large, round leaves on 1m (3ft) stems. Good autumn colour and great reflections.

Matteuccia struthiopteris (shuttlecock fern)
Stunning fern with plume-like foliage, for damp soil in sun.

Primula japonica (candelabra primula)
Stems of 'tiered' reddish-purple flowers, 75cm (2$\frac{1}{2}$ft) tall, in early summer.

Hostas
Great foliage, especially Hosta sieboldiana *for its big, bold, architectural, blue-green leaves.*

MAINTENANCE

Spring Mulch with a layer of rich organic matter every year such as well-rotted garden compost – this is vital, as you can't use fertilizers near a pond. Cut dogwoods close to ground level every spring to encourage colourful young stems, and divide overgrown bog plants every three to four years.

Summer Weed regularly. Control slugs with natural methods – don't use slug pellets in the bog garden or anywhere near the pond (in case a dead slug drops into the water). Frogs and hedgehogs will clear a lot of pests. Sprinkle sharp gravel round hostas to make it difficult for slugs to approach the plants. Use empty half-orange skins, placed upside down on the soil: slugs and snails collect in them and you can then just throw them away.

Autumn Cut back dead stems of herbaceous plants, but don't over-tidy as wildlife will need somewhere to spend the winter in safety. This is especially important if your bog garden is near a wildlife pond.

1 If you want a pond and a bog garden, dig and prepare both at the same time, leaving a ridge of soil between the pond and the bog to keep them separate. My suggested construction technique for the bog ensures that there is no risk at all of any soil being washed into the pond.

2 Make the pond as described on page 40, using a butyl liner.

3 Dig out the area for the bog: 30cm (1ft) deep if you want to grow only small plants like hostas and primulas, 45cm (1$\frac{1}{2}$ft) deep for larger perennials, or 75cm (2$\frac{1}{2}$ft) for dogwoods and gunnera.

4 Line the bottom half of the bog area with 5cm (2in) of sand, followed by pond liner (PVC is fine in this instance: once buried, it is out of the sunlight). Lining only the bottom half allows excess water to spill over and run away in wet weather. In a good bog garden the soil always stays moist but firm enough to walk on.

5 Fill the bog area with a mixture of soil and organic matter. Plant with your chosen plants and water thoroughly to dampen the soil well without making it marshy. Continue to water if rain does not keep the soil damp enough.

Pond

Soil and organic matter

Top edge of PVC liner

Soil ridge

Sand

fibreglass shell pond

A vast range of fibreglass pond shapes is on sale in garden centres and other outlets. They are hugely popular and can be a good way of making a pond, though there is a limited number of shapes and sizes. When constructed so that they are wholly or partly above the ground, they make very good features for patio or courtyard gardens, and are also an easy way of making the 'top pond' of a cascade down a rockery or the header for a stream. Unfortunately they can be pricey. Expect to pay about twice the price for a fibreglass shell shape as for the best butyl liner. Put in properly, a shell can last up to twenty-five years, as fibreglass does not become brittle through exposure to sunlight. But it is essential that the pond goes in perfectly level, otherwise you end up with all the water down at one end, which is difficult to correct. This is the trade secret for getting perfect results.

⏱ TIME

Three days.

🧒 CHILD FRIENDLY

No.

✋ MAINTENANCE

High.

💰 COST

About £280.

💧 YOU WILL NEED

- Preformed fibreglass pond shell 1.8 × 1.2m × 46cm deep (6 × 4 × 1½ft deep)
- Damp soft builder's sand
- Paving slabs and cement mix
- Water lily: 1
- Oxgenating plants: 10
- Marginal plants: 6

1 Start by roughly levelling and marking out the area. Use the preformed pond as a guide – stand it on the ground and trickle sand round it, then remove the shell to leave the outline shape. Dig the hole, following the contours of the pond exactly, but make it 30cm (1ft) wider all round. Make the hole 5cm (2in) deeper than the shell and firm the base well.

2 Cover the bottom of the hole with a 5cm (2in) layer of soft sand. From this moment onwards it is vital to get everything really level, so check the edges of the hole and adjust the soil level if necessary. Sit the pond shell in place. Then fill it with 7.5cm (3in) of water and leave it standing overnight to see if it shifts.

3 If it is still level next morning, back-fill round the shell shape with soil *only* as far as the planting shelf for the moment. Pack the soil well under the planting shelf, otherwise it will collapse as there is nothing to hold it up and the fibreglass will crack, making the pond leak. Keep a spirit level on a plank over the top of the pond all this time and check the level constantly. Then put more water in, up

to the shelf level, and leave the shell overnight to see if there is any settlement. If there is, take the water out, lift the shell and pack sand underneath at the appropriate point. Repeat all the previous steps.

4 Continue packing soil round the shell until it is level with the rim. Conceal the liner by paving the edges as on page 29 and add the plants.

Rocks or paving slabs hide edge of liner

Planting shelf

Sand

charlie's way with shell ponds

You don't have to bury a shell pond to its rim in the ground. I like to put this type of pond only half-way in, so that the planting shelf rests on the ground surface. This means a lot less digging (especially as the pond shape widens out above shelf level), but it also makes it easier to ensure the shelf is properly supported by the soil. Then just build up with rockwork or bricks and pack the gaps between the two with soil.

charlie says . . .

It's tempting to take short-cuts when installing this sort of pond, but don't. A lot of people make the mistake of digging the hole only the same size as the shell, and just dropping it in. This gives you no chance to pack the soil down hard all round it, so some of the soil sinks after a time. If this happens, the pond cracks, as it holds a huge weight of water which needs to be evenly supported – a shell shape cannot flex like a rubber liner. Shells can also crack if they are jammed into a hole that is a bit too small causing the fibreglass to bend.

RAISED PONDS

Raised ponds have a 'designer' look that particularly suits them to a modern garden. They are a good way to add height to a level area and because they are raised, the fish and plants are closer to the eye. One added advantage is that a raised pond on its own involves no major excavation, so you won't be left with large amounts of soil to dispose of.

A raised pond provides a good focal point in a 'garden room', and on a patio this type of water feature is extra-good value as you can sit and enjoy it, especially if you make the edges wide enough to sit on. Just cap the sides with paving slabs and bring out cushions on nice days so that you can watch the fish in comfort or just sunbathe. It's a good idea to plan a raised pond with paving and seating in mind, since, in practice, people always find they spend a lot longer sitting by the water than they anticipated.

Raised ponds are definitely formal features – they don't really lend themselves to 'wilder looking' schemes. That does not mean they have to be complicated: very much the reverse. They can be quite simple, just water and a few plants, so you don't necessarily need a pump or an electric supply. Various self-assembly kits are available if you want a really easy-to-construct project. But raised ponds also give you the opportunity to be quite creative. For instance, a formal, rectangular one can be the 'header tank' for a bigger project involving tumbling water cascading into a sunken pond. This is a good idea if you have a very flat garden, where a rockery and waterfall might look rather out of place. It could also form the basis of a big, adventurous project like the water pavement we showed on one *Ground Force* programme – but that is something for an experienced pond constructor, so wait until you have three or four ponds under your belt before tackling something so big.

Constructionally a raised pond can be a little more complicated than many types of water feature, as the walls need to be strong enough to hold a large volume of water: the water pressure can be quite great. Maintenance is much the same as for a sunken pond; it all depends on what you put in it. But if it has high sides a raised pond is more child-friendly than a sunken one –

at least, until the child is agile enough to climb up and over. On the minus side, birds and wildlife will not be able to make use of it.

One thing you need to think about is winter care. A tiny raised pond will freeze solid, so you need to make some provision for draining it – the empty shape could then be used to house pots of winter-flowering pansies and small evergreens. But a reasonable-sized pond surrounded by thick walls may be quite well insulated – especially if the base is sunk a few centimetres or so into the ground – and therefore immune to this problem.

FAR LEFT: *The wide edges of this lily pool are an ideal place to stand containers.*

LEFT: *Pebble pools are child-friendly as they contain only a shallow depth of water.*

BELOW: *A fun spouting fish adds interest to these linked ponds.*

raised
tank
pond

This raised container is very versatile. On its own, with no waterfall or pump, it would make a good free-standing feature for a formal garden with just one spectacular plant in it, like my favourite *Peltandra virginica*, which has big, tropical-looking leaves and green 'arum lily' flowers. But if you fancy the waterfall (and it is attractive), make a formal-shaped pond sunk into the ground for it to spill into. On *Ground Force* we made a water pavement, but a formal-shaped pond would be very attractive and much quicker and easier to construct.

LIGHTING THE WATER FEATURE

Lighting is great fun and really brings a moving water feature to life. For the TV programme we bought a lighting kit containing the cable and three 24-volt fully waterproof lights. One underwater light is in the tank and another at the base of the sluice where most of the water movement takes place. A third light went up a nearby tree, illuminating this part of the garden generally. This type of lighting kit is very easy to use. The lights simply clip on to the cable. We ran the power cable through the borders to the house, where we drilled through the house wall to get to a power point. The lights and pump were plugged in via a circuit breaker, with a transformer for the lights.

TIME

Three days to make the raised pond, allowing time for the cement to set, etc; allow five days in total if you also make a lower pond with paving round it.

CHILD FRIENDLY

No.

MAINTENANCE

Low.

COST

About £250.

YOU WILL NEED

For a raised pond 1m × 60cm × 38cm deep (3 × 2ft × 15in deep) plus sunken pond 1.8 × 1.2m × 60cm deep (6 × 4 × 2ft deep)

Raised pond
- Butyl liner 1.7 × 1.4m (5½ × 4½ft)
- Breeze blocks
- Flat natural walling stones
- Coping stones
- Cement mix
- Damp soft builder's sand
- Gravel
- 2 sheets of verdigris copper 18 × 38cm (7 × 15in)
- Thin copper wire
- Silicon sealant
- *Carex* 'Bowles Golden': 1 in planting basket

Sunken pond
- Butyl liner 3 × 2.4m (10 × 8ft)
- Damp soft builder's sand
- Paving slabs and cement mix
- Submersible pump with cable (450–550 gallons per hour)
- Conduit for cable and circuit breaker

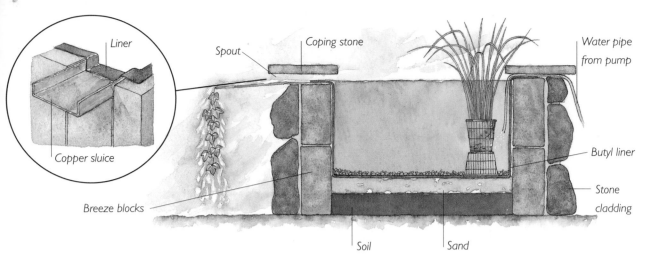

Liner

Spout

Coping stone

Water pipe
from pump

Copper sluice

Butyl liner

Stone
cladding

Breeze blocks

Soil

Sand

1 Make the sunken pond as on page 32. It should be at least twice the size of the raised tank. Put the pump into the deepest part of it and lay on electricity as described on page 14. Pave round the edges of the pond as described on page 29.

2 For the raised tank, use breeze blocks to make a box-shaped container. Stand the blocks on edge and cement them together, checking that each one is level as it is laid. When the cement has dried, make a gap for the spout by chiselling out a slot 13 × 4cm (5 × 1½in).

3 Cement flat, natural walling stones to the outside of the breeze blocks. Spread 7.5cm (3in) of soil over the base of the container to raise it above ground level, then spread 5cm (2in) of builder's sand as a cushion before lining it with butyl pond liner.

ABOVE LEFT: *Cementing together the breeze blocks for the raised tank.*

LEFT: *The copper leaves are simple to make and are a terrific finishing touch.*

4 To make the spout for water to run down from the reservoir, take a flat sheet of verdigris copper about 18 × 38cm (7 × 15in), put marks 2.5cm (1in) in from the two long sides with a pencil, and hammer the edges over the side of a block of wood to make a shallow lip. Cut leaf shapes from another sheet of copper; these will hang over the edge of the sluice so the water runs down them, instead of making a continuous sheet of water. For the *Ground Force* project we chose maple leaf shapes about 5 × 5cm (2 × 2in) big.

5 Slot the copper chute into place. Bring the end of the pond liner up out of the tank and use silicon to stick it 5cm (2in) from the end of the copper chute, making a watertight seal.

6 Fill the container with water, leaving the surplus liner hanging over the edge. Once the liner is fully weighted down by the water, trim off the edge. Then cement coping stones round the edge of the container to hide the edge of the liner. The stones

continue over the top of the sluice, leaving an opening for the water but hiding the join between the copper sluice and liner.

7 Hang the leaves from lengths of thin copper wire where the water overflows so that they make a gentle tinkling sound like a watery wind chime. Run the wires right back to the point where the copper chute joins the liner and stick in place with silicon. Put a thin layer of gravel in the base of the container to hide any creases in the liner and make the container look more natural.

8 Hiding the pipes can be tricky. The water-feed from the pump in the sunken pond comes in at the back of the raised pond under a coping stone so you can't see it. For extra concealment, place a potted marginal plant in front of it. On the *Ground Force* programme we used one *Carex* 'Bowles Golden' (Bowles' golden sedge) in a planting basket.

hexagonal
pond with
fountain

This geometric-shaped pond would look particularly good as the centrepiece to a formal garden, or you could put it on the patio. It is an incredibly quick and easy project; you literally just buy all the 'ingredients' and fit them together. The pond itself is made from a kit that is easily assembled. The fountain is in the form of a cherub with a birdbath and fountain already fitted – just stand it in the middle of the pond and attach it to the pump. You could complete the project even faster if you did not want a fountain, as about a third of the total construction time is taken up by laying on power.

TIME

Half a day.

CHILD FRIENDLY

No.

MAINTENANCE

Low.

COST

About £200 (not including the paving base).

YOU WILL NEED

For a hexagonal pond about 1m (3ft) in diameter

- Ready-to-lay circle of paving slabs about 1.8m (6ft) in diameter
- Cement mix
- Self-assembly hexagonal pond kit
- Water-based wood stain
- Screws
- Fountain
- Clean terracotta plant pots:2
- Submersible pump with cable
- Conduit for cable
- Circuit breaker

1 Lay an electric power cable to the pond site as described on page 14.

2 Lay a circle of paving slabs on a bed of cement ensuring that they are perfectly level. Some makers sell sets of slabs ready-made to fit together to form a circle, so you don't need to do any cutting.

3 Paint the individual pieces of the pond kit using a water-based wood stain: we used a dark green colour called Holly, which is very popular now.

4 Screw together the pond rim (see below), place it on the paving base and stand the preformed pond shape inside it.

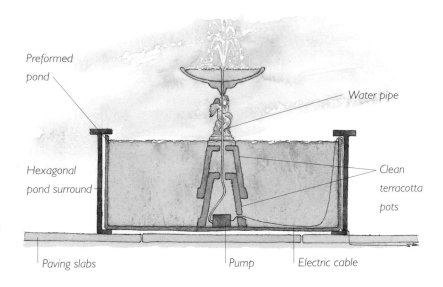

Preformed pond

Water pipe

Hexagonal pond surround

Clean terracotta pots

Paving slabs   Pump   Electric cable

5 Fit a submersible pump in the pond as described on page 15. You will need to raise the fountain up, so drill a hole in the side of a terracotta plant pot, place the pot over the pump and run the cable through the hole. Place another pot on top to form a pedestal.

6 Carefully place the fountain on top of the pedestal and connect it to the pump. Fill the pond with water.

as described on page 14. / as described on page 15.

charlie says . . .

If you wanted to create a fishpond, you would have to stand marginal plants on upturned planting baskets since there are no planting shelves in the pond. (This is much better than standing them on bricks, as you don't risk introducing bits of grit that might damage your pump.)

You would need about six oxygenating plants and up to six 5cm (2in) fish. But to avoid any residue from the coloured stain (which is water-based) affecting the fish, after painting the surround let it dry completely, then rinse it off well before putting in the liner and filling it with water.

modern canal

This modern version of a formal canal makes a small garden look bigger, as the mirror at the end reflects light back into the garden, creating an optical illusion that doubles the length of the canal. It looks terribly impressive, but isn't actually difficult to make. The hardest job is shifting the heavy sleepers — be sure that you have two people to move them. As you might expect, the canal suits a formal garden, but used obliquely as in the *Ground Force* programme, it creates a sensational focal point for a modern 'abstract' garden flanked by decking.

TIME
One day.

CHILD FRIENDLY
No.

MAINTENANCE
Medium.

COST
About £360.

YOU WILL NEED

For a canal 7 × 1.8m × 45cm deep
(23 × 6 × 1½ft deep)

- PVC or butyl liner 8 × 2.75m (26 × 9ft)
- Bonded fibre underlay 2.1 × 3m (7 × 10ft) cut into 30cm (1ft) lengths
- 8 wooden railway sleepers
- Mitred wooden boards about 25cm (10in) wide: about 21.3m (70ft) total length
- Dry-mix cement
- Metal strips about 15cm (6in) long with holes for screws
- Screws and nails
- Damp soft builder's sand
- Black paint
- Planting basket
- Submersible pump with cable
- Conduit for cable and circuit breaker
- Mirror and wooden frame
- 20mm- (³/₄in-)thick plywood

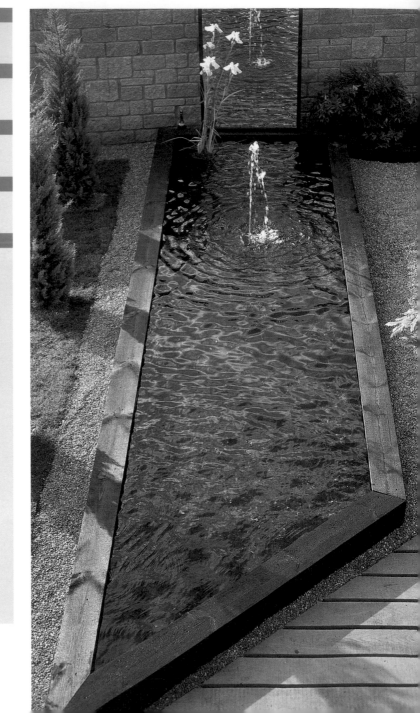

1 To make the edges of the canal, mark out its shape and dig a shallow, flat-bottomed trench, the same width as the sleepers, all round it. Our canal was an irregular shape, but a rectangular pond would be easier to construct and line.

2 Lay on electric power cable to the pond site as described on page 14.

3 Cut the sleepers to lengths that fit the sides of the canal, first checking them over for any nails which can make a chainsaw 'jump' and ruin the teeth of a handsaw. You can sometimes get sleepers precut for you, which saves a lot of time.

4 Put a layer of dry-mix cement in the trench, then lay the sleepers on top. Check that they are level and adjust if necessary. The cement draws up moisture from the damp soil and sets to give a perfect fit. Join the sleepers together from the inside of the canal using strips of metal about 15cm (6in) long with holes for screws.

5 Once the sleepers are in place, dig out 25cm (10in) of soil from inside the canal, leaving a firm, level bottom.

6 Cover the base of the canal with a 5cm (2in) layer of soft sand. Cover the sleeper sides with bonded fibre pond underlay to protect the liner from splinters, then lay a PVC or butyl liner.

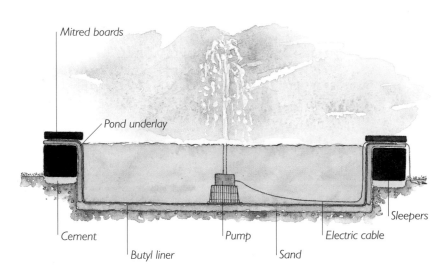

Mitred boards

Pond underlay

Cement

Butyl liner

Pump

Sand

Electric cable

Sleepers

7 Fill the canal with water, trim away the surplus liner and tack the edges down to the top of the sleepers with a few nails to hold the liner roughly in place.

8 Stand the pump in the centre of the canal on an upturned planting basket and bring the cable from the pump up and over the side. There is no need to fix a fountain jet to the top of the water outlet – the pump produces a formal jet of water. Hide the edge of the liner by nailing neatly mitred boards over the top of the sleepers. Paint both boards and sleepers black. Hide the cable for the pump: on the television programme we put it under the edge of the timber decking we built along the edge of the pond.

9 To make the mirror at the end of the canal, fix a glass mirror to a sheet of 20mm- ($\frac{3}{4}$in-)thick plywood cut to the same size as the glass, using a wooden frame to hold it in place. Attach this firmly to the fence or wall at the far end of the canal.

charlie says . . .

You could do more with this project, but keep it formal. You could create a classic canal, with a row of water lilies evenly spaced out along the middle. The fountain would have to be a low one to avoid splashing them. And if you want fish, dig the canal a bit deeper so that they have at least 45cm ($1\frac{1}{2}$ft) of water.

The canal we built was 7m (23ft) long, but you could easily adapt the instructions to make a shorter version which, with clever use of a mirror, could still 'add' metres to your garden.

rustic pole pond

Rustic poles form an unusual surround for this raised pond. By making them all different heights you can create an informal look which is just right for a modern house and garden. Because of the natural appearance of the poles the pond would also look good in a wildlife garden.

⏱ TIME
One and a half days.

🔤 CHILD FRIENDLY
Fairly.

✋ MAINTENANCE
Low.

💰 COST
About £250.

💧 YOU WILL NEED
For a pond 1.2m (4ft) in diameter and 46cm (1 ½ ft) deep
- Butyl liner 2.1 × 2.1m (7 × 7ft)
- Wooden fencing poles 1.5m (5ft) long
- Damp soft builder's sand
- Foam jet (see page 59)
- Tacks
- Screws, length 1½ times diameter of fencing poles
- Submersible pump with cable
- Conduit for cable and circuit breaker

1 To make the rustic pole pond surround, dig a circular hole 46cm (1½ft) deep with a flat base (see page 33 for how to mark out a circle), and hammer a ring of poles into the ground all round the edge. Cover the base with a 5cm (2in) layer of sand.

2 Drop butyl liner inside and gather the folds into small pleats to even them out neatly all round the inside of the pond, without making big folds. Fill with water and trim the liner roughly, then use tacks to fix it to the poles just above the water level.

3 The edge of the liner is hidden by the inner row of poles. These do not go the full depth of the pond, but only a few centimetres below the water level. They are held up by screws that fix them to the outer row of poles. (Use tanalized wood which won't rot.) Screw them at the top only, so as not to puncture the liner.

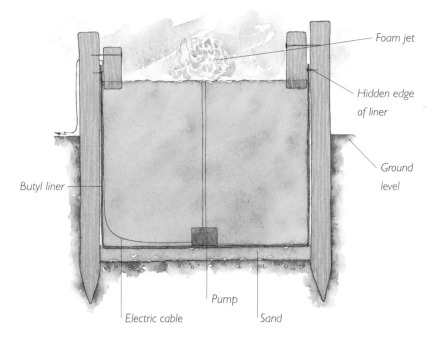

Foam jet

Hidden edge of liner

Ground level

Butyl liner

Electric cable

Pump

Sand

4 To give the pond its dramatic shape, cut the poles off at different heights to form a spiral shape, winding down from 1m (3ft) to 30cm (1ft) above the ground. The water level is 10cm (4in) down from the top of the lowest post, so it is still about 20cm (8in) above ground level.

5 Sit the pump in the bottom of the pond and fit a foam jet to the water outlet. Run the electric cable from the pump up and over the liner between the inner and outer rings of poles, and away to the power supply in the house (see page 14).

charlie says . . .

In the Ground Force *programme we did not use any plants in the pond. But next to it we planted a dome-shaped miniature pine, an evergreen grass (Festuca glauca), some euonymus and a phormium, which will look good all year round. There was a big, shiny-trunked Prunus serrula nearby, and Alan planted pampas grass (see right) to make an attractive fountain effect in the opposite corner of the garden.*

FOUNTAINS

A fountain not only looks nice, it is actually good for a pond as it 'forces' lots of oxygen to dissolve in the water more. This benefits fish — one reason why playing a fountain helps distressed fish on hot, sultry summer mornings — and can help improve the ecological balance of the pond.

The fountain effect is made by a special jet that fits to the outlet on the top of a submersible pump. You don't have to use a jet at all — you will get a nice ripple of water by just leaving the top of the pump 'bare' of accessories — but spray jets do look nice. There are dozens of kinds, formal and informal. You can have spinning spray heads, foaming gushers and even coloured lights. But to look right a fountain must be in the correct style for its surroundings and match the size and scale of the pond.

BLOCKED JETS

The biggest problem with fountains is blocked jets. Always put a fountain where it is easy to get at as you'll need to sort this one out fairly often. When jets block, poke the dirt out of the holes with a straightened paperclip or pull off the rose and clean it out under a tap, according to type. You can help prevent blocked jets by choosing a foam jet as this has big holes, or using a pump with a pre-filter to sieve out debris — though you will need to clean the filter.

Fountains In Ponds

✔ *Do choose a fountain that is less than half the diameter of the pond.*

✘ *Don't try to grow water lilies under a fountain: they won't grow if the leaves are always getting splashed.*

✔ *Do think of the noise if you are going to leave a fountain running all the time.*

✘ *Don't have a fountain in a windy site.*

✔ *Do adjust the height of a fountain by turning down the flow using a little tap in the side of the pump (see left).*

ABOVE AND RIGHT: *Fountains can look lovely in small gardens. Use them to brighten up a dull corner or to add a formal touch to a small pond.*

Which Fountain?

Rose fountain *My favourite, giving a traditional spray made up of several tiers of fine droplets.*

Bubble jet fountain *A very quiet fountain, and perfect for pebble pools or in a container pond.*

Gusher jet *Makes a spectacular jet like a geyser; this is the noisiest fountain of all, and sounds like a rushing waterfall.*

Bell jet fountain *Makes a low, wide, bell-shaped wall of water, ideal for pebble pools. Very quiet, but often blocks, leaving you with only half a bell – and in a windy spot it looks like an out-of-control crinoline skirt!*

Tulip fountain *Like a bell, but a more pointed shape.*

Spray rings *Make a formal, Versailles-style fountain, forming a jelly-mould shape of moving water.*

Foam jet *Makes a 'head' rather like the froth on a pint of beer, which is caused by the holes in the sides that suck in air and mix it with the water, so you get a greater oxygenating effect than usual. Of all fountains this is the type that blocks up least frequently and is the least affected by windy conditions. Large intake holes mean a foam jet needs a bigger water throughput and therefore a more powerful pump to run it.*

Rose fountain

Bell jet fountain

Tulip fountain

Foam jet

BUBBLE FOUNTAINS

Bubble fountains are so-called because
the water bubbles up from a hole in a
large rock or over stones. The best-known
are those that feature a grindstone or
large rock with a hole drilled through the
middle, where the water trickles away
into a carpet of pebbles all round the
edge. But you can convert all sorts of
decorative items holding as little as
$\frac{1}{2}$ gallon (2.25 litres) of water to make
your own unique fountain.

A bubble fountain is one of the most creative kinds of water feature, and looks most at home in modern surroundings. It is the sort to choose if you enjoy the sound of running water, but don't have the time to make or maintain a pond.

What is special about a bubble fountain is that it has no standing water – the reservoir is an underground container. This makes it perfectly safe for a garden where there are small children, and good for a front garden where there is open access: no one is suddenly going to land in a metre of cold water. Yet wildlife can still drink and bathe in the 'splash zone'. And as the water makes only the gentlest burbling sound, a bubble fountain is soothing with no risk of disturbing the neighbours. You can make one just about anywhere there is room – even in a container.

Regardless of what you use on top of the bubble fountain, underneath it is a central sump with a sloping flange all round, so water runs back into the reservoir. Projects can be quite simple, using a preformed pebble pool base that just needs dropping into a hole in the ground. But for more elaborate projects using something

heavy like a grindstone, you often need a bigger underground reservoir and extra reinforcing to support the weight.

Of course, since all the water is underground you can't have fish or water plants with this type of feature. But because the water spends most of its time in the dark it is less likely to go green. Furthermore, as there are no fish or plants in this type of feature, you can keep both the water and the pebbles perfectly clean by adding an algicide to the reservoir.

You do not need any special jets to create the fountain, as the normal water outlet at the top of the pump does the job nicely. And although you cannot have plants in the water feature, you can make up for it by growing good structural ones like grasses, irises or bamboos around the outside.

FAR LEFT: This classical jar is easy to maintain and would look lovely in a Mediterranean-style garden.
LEFT: Water gathers in the base of this leaf fountain forming a pool where birds can come and bathe.
BELOW: A traditional grindstone fountain looks beautiful in almost any part of the garden.

drilled rock fountain

Perfect for any slightly quirky, minimalist style of garden, this feature also looks wonderful surrounded by slabs on a patio, or in a wild garden. It is quick and easy to make because it uses a preformed plastic pebble pool base. These devices have revolutionized water features, bringing them within the grasp of even the most ham-fisted DIYer. They are perfect for us on *Ground Force* as they take so little time to install.

TIME

Three hours.

CHILD FRIENDLY

Yes.

MAINTENANCE

Negligible.

COST

About £160.

YOU WILL NEED

- Drilled rock
- Preformed pebble pool base
- Damp soft builder's sand
- Cobbles
- Submersible pump with cable
- Conduit for cable and circuit breaker

You will find preformed pebble pool bases in your local water garden centre and they can sometimes be found in DIY outlets and ordinary garden centres. They're perfect for the modern garden as they are low maintenance and also very fashionable. To make life even easier, some garden centres sell complete water feature kits which contain everything you need in one package. The only extra things you need to buy are the cobbles to conceal the reservoir once it's in place.

1 Dig a hole for the preformed pebble pool base, line it with sand, then lower the base into place, making sure that it is perfectly level. (It looks like an upturned hat with the brim firmly supported by the soil underneath.) Sit the pump on the bottom of the reservoir. Meanwhile organize the electric supply (see page 14).

2 Roll the drilled rock into the centre of the plastic base. It is wider than the reservoir, so it rests on the brim, with the weight supported by the soil underneath. Roll the rock over slightly and jam the hosepipe leading off the pump firmly up into the hole in the base of the rock. Coil the spare hose round inside the reservoir, leaving enough slack to manoeuvre as you lower the rock back in place. This way, if you need to get at the pump for any reason in future, it is very easy to do so.

3 Fill the reservoir with water and leave the fountain running for an hour so you can check that the water runs back into the reservoir. If it spills over the edge into the soil, it will soon empty the reservoir. Only when you are sure everything is OK do you put the cobbles round the feature to hide the plastic base.

charlie says . .

If the water runs out only over one side of the rock, it's either because the rock is not level or because the hole has been drilled through it at an angle, so the water is not coming out straight. The easy remedy is to jam bits of thin slate under the rock to level it. Do this with the fountain running so you can see where the water runs – then you know exactly where to tuck the slate to get an even spread.

When you are buying a drilled rock to make a water feature, choose a boulder which has a small borehole in one side to take the hosepipe, and a larger hole drilled through from the top to meet it. (It's usually the bigger rocks that are drilled like this – see those in the picture below.) This way, the water fills a depression, wells up over the side and overflows gently instead of squirting out.

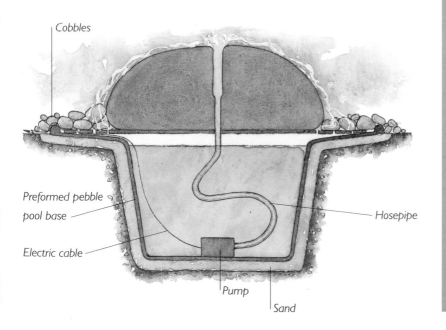

Cobbles

Preformed pebble pool base

Electric cable

Hosepipe

Pump

Sand

bubbling ali baba jar

⏱ **TIME**

One day.

♿ **CHILD FRIENDLY**

Fairly.

✋ **MAINTENANCE**

Negligible.

💰 **COST**

About £300.

💧 **YOU WILL NEED**

- Large terracotta Ali Baba jar about 1m (3ft) tall and 227 litres (50 gallons) capacity
- Butyl liner 2.1 × 1.8m (7 × 6ft)
- Strong metal bars 75 × 25mm × 1.8m long (3 × 1in × 6ft long)
- Metal grid 1.2 × 61cm (4 × 2ft)
- Board
- Large smooth pebbles, small stones/gravel
- Damp soft builder's sand
- Submersible pump with cable
- Conduit for cable and circuit breaker
- Thick flexible hosepipe
- Metal spigot
- Silicon sealant and rustproofing paint
- *Hakonechloa macra* 'Aureola': 3 in pots

This is another of those terribly useful, go-anywhere features that always looks absolutely brilliant – use it on a patio, in a formal garden, with gravel or with cobbles in a border. It suits both contemporary and minimalist, oriental-inspired and Mediterranean styles. A slightly different form of pebble fountain, it uses an overflowing terracotta jar. But, in just the same way as in the grindstone and drilled-rock types, the water runs down the side of the jar and disappears through pebbles to be recycled from a reservoir hidden away underneath. The textured pattern on the side of the jar makes the water ripple a bit as it trickles down over the edge instead of running straight down.

1 Dig a hole for the sump with a shallow dished shelf on one side. The shelf will form the pebbley puddle at the side of the jar. Stand a board on its side on the inside of the dish to form a lip which will keep the pebbles where you want them. Organize the electricity supply (see page 14).

2 Line the hole with sand and put in a butyl liner (see page 32), laying it over the top of the board.

3 Sit the pump on the base of the sump. Attach a piece of thick hosepipe to the water outlet: this will lead to a hole in the base of the jar.

4 Since the jar will be very heavy when full, you will need to support it with several strong metal bars. Paint both the bars and the metal grid, which will support the pebbles surrounding the jar, with rustproofing paint and allow to dry. Lay the bars over the hole: they should protrude 46cm (1½ft) on each side.

5 Lay the grid on top of the bars: it should protrude 15cm (6in) all round the hole. Feed the hosepipe up through the grid. Cut the grid away over the dished shelf and run pebbles down to the concealed board. When these are covered with water, the jar will stand in a pebbley puddle on one side, while on the other, the stones covering the grid will be splashed by the water cascading down the side.

6 Set the jar on the grid. Feed the hosepipe through the hole in the base of the jar and seal it to the metal spigot, which should rise up through the middle so that its top reaches just below the rim. Using silicon, seal round the point where the pipework passes through the base of the pot, so it does not leak. Put a few pebbles in the bottom of the jar to stabilize the spigot and add interest. Fill the jar with water and switch on the pump: as the water comes out of the spigot it should create a low, spreading ripple.

7 When you are sure that everything is working correctly and that the water is running back into the sump, cover the grid with pebbles and surround the jar with tufts of *Hakonechloa macra* 'Aureola' (stripy Japanese grass), mulched with cobbles, pebbles, gravel and sand.

VIEW FROM ABOVE

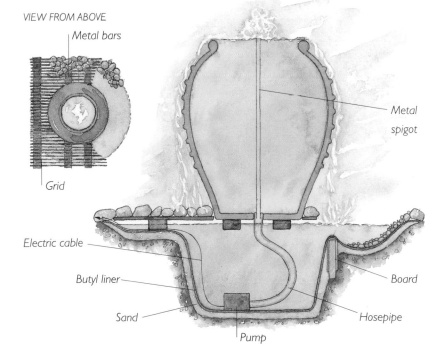

Metal bars

Grid

Metal spigot

Electric cable

Butyl liner

Board

Sand

Hosepipe

Pump

millstone bubble fountain

Like all bubble fountains this is very versatile and would look good as a centrepiece for a small formal garden or as a formal feature in a bigger garden, and would be equally at home on a patio or in a contemporary gravel or pebble feature. A garden classic, it would also suit a more traditional-style family garden, perhaps flanked by a shrubbery.

TIME

One day.

CHILD FRIENDLY

Yes.

MAINTENANCE

Negligible.

COST

About £350.

YOU WILL NEED

- Circular 'millstone' with central hole
- Circular black plastic tank about 30cm (1ft) deep
- breeze blocks: 9
- Decorative copper flower
- Bell jet fountain
- Damp soft builder's sand
- Cobbles and pebbles
- Silicon sealant
- Submersible pump with cable
- Conduit for cable
- Circuit breaker

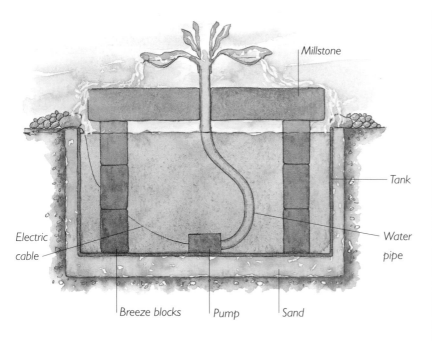

Millstone

Tank

Water pipe

Electric cable

Breeze blocks

Pump

Sand

A real grindstone was well beyond the *Ground Force* budget, so we economized and used a circular stone table-top instead. It already had a hole through the middle, which had originally been intended to take a sunshade. The reservoir is a circular black plastic tank, about 30cm (1ft) deep, from a DIY shop. Our 'stone' fitted almost exactly over the tank with only a 2.5cm (1in) gap round the edge for the water to run back into the tank.

1 Dig a hole in the ground about the same size as the tank with a firm, level base, line it with sand, then sink the tank into it. Pack extra sand round the sides to make a tight fit. As always, use a spirit level to check that this is perfectly level as you work.

2 Install the electric cable as described on page 14. Place the pump in the tank.

3 Sit the circular stone in place just above the tank, supported by three piles of three breeze blocks, with its central hole over the pipe from the pump. Check it with a spirit level, then, using silicon sealant, seal the hole round the pipe where it comes through the middle of the stone.

4 Fit a bell jet fountain to the water outlet on the pump and hide it with a decorative copper flower. Fill the tank with water and switch on the pump. The water trickles up through the middle of the flower and then cascades down the petals and out over the edges of the stone circle, where it runs gently back into the tank beneath.

5 Surround the feature with cobbles and pebbles.

raised leaf fountain

This spectacular leaf fountain makes a very unusual and stunning centrepiece in a tiny, formal courtyard garden in a town, in the midst of a scented garden. The shallow pool created in the middle of the leaf attracts birds to drink and bathe. You would hardly know you were in a city centre! In larger-scale surroundings you could sit it in a shrub border for a more natural look, or put it in a contemporary garden surrounded by pebbles. I'd like to see it used as an architectural feature next to a very natural-looking pond. You could even get away with it in a wildlife garden, flanked by wild flowers.

The fibreglass gunnera leaf we used on the *Ground Force* programme was a one-off life-size sculpture 1.5m (5ft) across – but you could create your own unique water feature by adapting anything similar that holds 2.27 litres (½ gallon) of

TIME
Two hours.

CHILD FRIENDLY
Yes.

MAINTENANCE
Negligible.

COST
About £200.

YOU WILL NEED
- Fibreglass sculpture
- Bricks
- Cement mix
- Silicon sealant
- Small submersible pump with cable
- Conduit for cable
- Circuit breaker

water at its lowest point. For this you will need only a very small pump like the one described on page 26. A leaf sculpture will not have a flat base, so you need to make a hollow brick pier for it to sit on. The pointed base will fit into the pier and will be bedded into cement. Cement does not stick to fibreglass, but forms a mould shape that the base rests in. You can then lift the sculpture out to clean it when necessary.

SURROUNDING PLANTING

The surrounding planting consists of a narrow border of shade-tolerant plants, including ferns and hostas planted around the base of the pier. The fountain is seen against a background of herringbone bricks that floor the courtyard area, with creeping thymes planted in some of the cracks. Other scented plants like lavender and sages surround the paving, and at the far end of the garden is the arbour where you can sit and enjoy the view. The gunnera leaf was the one big extravagance in the *Ground Force* garden.

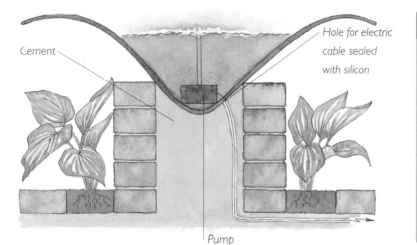

Cement

Hole for electric cable sealed with silicon

Pump

charlie says . . .

An alternative is to fill the hollow brick plinth with gravel instead of cement. Then you can move the sculpture about until the pump stands upright – otherwise the fountain always squirts a bit to one side. This is an easier option, particularly if you're not very confident about getting the position of the sculpture right first time.

1 Make a hollow brick pier, 45–60cm (1½–2ft) high, to support the sculpture.

2 Drill through the leaf near its lowest point to make a hole for the power cable from the pump to pass through. From there run the cable down through the hollow plinth and out under the surrounding paving back to the house as described on page 14.

3 Fill the hollow plinth with cement. Rest the leaf on the plinth and seal the tiny gap between the cable and the edge of the hole with silicon so that the leaf will not leak later.

4 Sit the pump in the centre of the leaf, which forms a natural 'basin' shape and will make the reservoir for the pump. Fill the leaf with water and set the pump to low, so that it makes a very pleasing ripple that just disturbs the water.

WALL-MOUNTED FEATURES

*A wall-mounted fountain makes a great
feature for a formal garden, where there are
a lot of hard surfaces. It is a good way to
create interest in a long expanse of dull wall
and provides the perfect focal point for a
tiny patio or courtyard garden. Use one in
sun or shade, with or without plants, and
make it as plain or elaborate as you like.
You don't even need to dig a hole!*

Traditional wall-mounted features (LEFT AND RIGHT) *look beautiful but take time to install. If you want more instant results, many garden centres sell easy-to-assemble kits which give a similar effect* (FAR LEFT).

A traditional wall-mounted fountain consists of a tank standing on the ground, which holds the pump and water reserve, and an ornamental outlet fixed to the wall above it. Lions' heads are the traditional favourite, but you can also get spouting suns, winds, or a 'green man'. Normally the jet of water squirts straight into the tank, but for a fancier feature you can direct the jet into a shell-shaped 'basin' fixed half-way down the wall, which in turn overflows at three points into the reservoir. If you don't want something quite so traditional, you could make the wall fountain play into a pond sunk into the ground, or use a waterproofed stone trough or a sink instead of the usual rectangular tank. If so, make sure it catches all the water – some types of wall fountain splash a lot, and this would empty the reservoir in time. The traditional lion's head fountain has a very directional jet of water which does not make much splash, so this is the one to choose if you are using a non-standard reservoir. It is also a good choice if you want to stand plants in the tank. Simply place the plants where they are not right in the firing line, as none of them appreciates being squirted constantly and

even the toughest marginals can scorch if this happens in strong sunlight.

HIDING THE PIPES

Between the fountain head, where the water comes out, and the tank containing the pump is the pipework connecting the two. This is where the big problem with wall-mounted fountains arises, as you do not want to see pipes running up the wall. One solution is to drill through the wall and take the pipes up the other side and out again near the top. This is fine if it is an ordinary garden wall, but not possible if – as usually happens – you want your fountain on the side of the house. The result would be pipes running up your living room wall. One alternative is to hide them under some form of wall decoration, or to make the pipes themselves look ornamental. But the simplest solution is to buy a wall-mounted fountain kit complete with bowl, mask, fountain, reservoir and pump all contained in a single one-piece unit which you just hang on the wall. All you need do is drill a hole through the wall behind it for the cable to run to the power supply.

lion's head fountain

For this *Ground Force* programme we took a tiny back garden with a minute paved area by the back door and turned it into a glamorous, burnt-orange, Tuscan-style patio complete with a grapevine-clad pergola which had, as its centrepiece, this lion's head wall fountain. The very decorative, black metal tank was actually rescued from a scrapyard and cost next to nothing, though we did have to do a bit of restoration work on it. Still, it just shows what you can do with imaginative recycling! Remember that you don't have to follow our ideas to the letter. You can adapt the project to suit your own preferences – and whatever your recycling instincts suggest. The symmetrical look of the fountain would also fit well into a formal garden, where it would be a good way to introduce some detail and movement into a long stretch of boring wall, or it would make an interesting 'hidden' feature to discover in a shady corner of a rambling, 'overgrown', natural-style garden.

TIME
One and a half days.

CHILD FRIENDLY
Fairly.

MAINTENANCE
Low.

COST
About £150.

YOU WILL NEED
- Lion's head wall fountain
- Second-hand decorative galvanized metal tank
- Second-hand pantiles
- Lead flashing
- Wooden battens
- Screws and rawlplugs
- Black bitumastic paint
- Submersible pump with cable
- Conduit for cable
- Circuit breaker

charlie says...

We didn't use any plants for this particular project, but at home I like to stand one or two pots of good marginal water plants in a wall fountain's tank – they make a nice contrast with all the hard surfaces around them. Tall, upright plants look best. Cyperus longus or Scirpus zebrinus are a good choice, and the two go well together. Stand the pots on a small upturned planting basket if the water is too deep for them (right).

1 Scrape any loose rust off the old tank (wear goggles to protect your eyes), then paint the inside only with black bitumastic paint. While it is drying, drill through the house wall so that the power cable from the fountain can be plugged into an electric socket indoors (see page 14).

2 Stand the tank in place and screw wooden battens to the wall above it. These will support the tiles that hide the water pipe going up from the tank to the lion's head. Use rawlplugs for the screws to create a firmer support. Leave a vertical gap for the pipe to fit into. Sit the pump in the tank and fit the water pipe into the gap between the battens.

3 Screw old pantiles to the battens, one batten for each row of tiles, so that they overlap like tiles on a roof. Finish off by fitting a strip of lead flashing to hide the upper edge of the top row of tiles.

4 Hang the lion's head in the middle of the top row of tiles, push the pipe through the mouth and then fill the tank with water. Switch on the pump.

5 Adjust the water flow going through the pump (there's a small 'tap' in the side of the pump housing to do this with) so that the water squirts neatly into the tank, not out over the side.

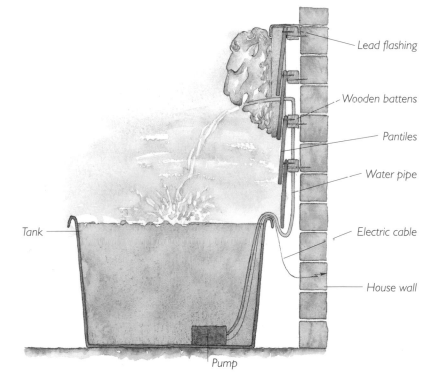

Lead flashing

Wooden battens

Pantiles

Water pipe

Electric cable

House wall

Tank

Pump

STREAMS

A stream is a great way to extend the water theme all round the garden. It makes the perfect excuse for adding fascinating 'extras' like cascades or waterfalls and watery 'props' such as rustic bridges, pebbly banks and waterside plants en route. In character a stream is a very informal or even positively wild feature. Don't make it too straight – it should meander about. Ideally you would landscape it into a natural depression in the ground where water tends to collect anyway. Being shallow, a stream attracts lots of wildlife to the garden besides being very child-friendly.

One of the most successful ways of using a stream is to have it running into a pond, or use it to link two ponds together. To get a natural look, make sure the bed of the stream isn't too level.

To landscape the banks of a stream, choose marginal plants that can stand gently moving water. Opt for the most compact but pretty waterside native species for a very natural stream, perhaps running into a wildlife pond, and use those plus cultivated versions for an

ornamental stream. And if you want something interesting to grow in the stream itself, try *Nymphoïdes peltata* (pond fringe). This is a native plant with 5cm (2in) wide, floating, heart-shaped leaves and broad, yellow flowers. Water lilies are not suitable as they hate moving water. But whatever you grow, make sure that the plants don't block the flow of the stream. This can cause the water to run out over the edge of the liner and the stream will run dry.

FAR LEFT: *The slate used to construct this small cascade gives the effect of a rocky mountain stream.*

LEFT: *Make sure the bed of your stream isn't too level. When the pump is turned off, water will collect in the 'pockets' forming pools where birds can bathe.*

ABOVE: *If you have an uneven garden, make the most of a natural depression by creating a winding stream.*

SURFACE PUMPS

If you have a long stream of 10–12m (35–40ft) or more, a submersible pump will not be powerful enough, so use a surface pump instead. As the name suggests, this needs to sit on dry land, close to the lower pond, in a weatherproof house that permits air circulation, or perhaps in a handy shed.

small rocky cascade

This is an ideal beginner's project, as the construction is just like that of a stream, but on a small scale. Install it in an area of scree in the sloping side of a reasonable-sized rockery, so the water splashes down 'naturally'. If you have a sloping garden, you could make a sloping area of gravel planted with rock plants, at ground level, and use something like this to suggest a natural spring. Though it appears impressive, it is actually very easy to make if you already have the rockery. Creative cementing is the key!

TIME

One to two days (one day to make plus drying time for the cement).

CHILD FRIENDLY

Yes.

MAINTENANCE

Low.

COST

About £185.

YOU WILL NEED

For a cascade 1.8m (6ft) long and 30cm (1ft) wide plus a sunken pond 1m × 60cm × 45cm deep (3 × 2 × 1¹/₂ft deep)

Cascade
- Butyl liner 2.1m × 91cm (7 × 3ft)
- Damp soft builder's sand
- Cement mix
- Pebbles and stones
- Hosepipe 2.5cm (1in) in diameter

Sunken pond
- Butyl liner 1.8 × 1.5m (6 × 5ft)
- Damp soft builder's sand
- 2 plastic feature grids
- Submersible pump with cable
- Conduit for cable
- Circuit breaker

charlie says . . .

Don't try to put a stream on a steep slope. If you have a hilly garden, make a waterfall that feeds into a stream running through level ground. Or use a cascade that takes advantage of the lie of the land.

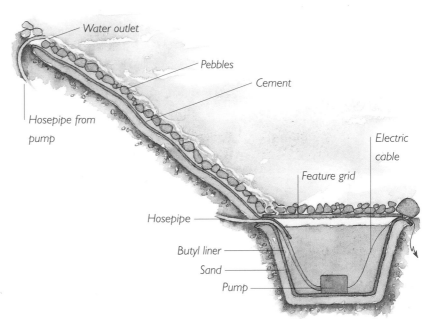

Water outlet

Pebbles

Cement

Hosepipe from pump

Electric cable

Feature grid

Hosepipe

Butyl liner

Sand

Pump

1 Dig a hole to make a reservoir about 1m × 60cm × 46cm deep (3 × 2 × 1½ft deep) at the base of the rockery. Line with sand and butyl liner as described on page 32.

2 Organize the electricity supply as described on page 14.

3 Line the course of the cascade with damp sand and butyl liner, ensuring that the butyl overlaps the reservoir liner.

4 Cover the cascade liner completely with mortar (made with 3 parts sand to 1 part cement) and push pebbles into it while it is still wet – the aim is to make it look exactly like the surrounding scree covering the rest of the rock garden.

5 Place the pump in the reservoir. Lay 2.5cm- (1in-)diameter hosepipe leading from the pump up

along the side of the cascade and position the outlet at the top so that water will flow down over the pebbles. These displace the water, so it does not just pour straight down the slope, but instead trickles gently around them, creating a very natural effect. Hide the hosepipe with stones.

6 Cover the reservoir with two feature grids. (These are either plastic or metal and are shaped like doormats: buy them from water garden specialists.) Conceal the grids with pebbles.

PLANTING

Use creeping rockery plants to soften the effect of a rock cascade like this. Many rockery plants are quite happy growing with the ends of their stems flopping into water, but for damp soil around the very edge of the cascade I recommend the variegated forget-me-not *Myosotis* 'Maytime'.

stream connecting two ponds

⊘ **TIME**

Seven days or more for construction; at least twenty days for cement to dry.

⊞ **CHILD FRIENDLY**

No.

✋ **MAINTENANCE**

High.

◉ **COST**

About £330.

◈ **YOU WILL NEED**

For a stream 3.7m (12ft) long and 61cm (2ft) wide linking an upper pond 1.8 × 1.2m (6 × 4ft) with a lower pond 2.7 × 1.8m × 61cm deep (9 × 6 × 2ft deep)

Stream
- PVC liner 4.3 × 1.2m (14 × 4ft)
- Damp soft builder's sand
- Mortar
- Rocks
- Liquid resin sealant
- Hosepipe 2.5cm (1in) in diameter

Lower pond
- Butyl liner 4 × 3m (13 × 10ft)
- Damp soft builder's sand
- Paving slabs and cement mix
- Submersible pump with cable
- Conduit for cable
- Circuit breaker

Upper pond
- Preformed fibreglass pond shell 1.8 × 1.2m (6 × 4ft)
- Damp soft builder's sand
- Fibreglass car-repair kit

This project offers plenty of extra opportunities for waterside planting *en route*. But a stream can also look great in any wild, wildlife or rock garden, or as a natural-looking feature in any informal style of garden.

Break the project down into its component parts. The top pond, made from a fibreglass pond shell, acts as the 'header tank', with a stream linking it to the butyl-lined lower pond which must be at least twice the size. Make the bottom pond first, then the stream and finally the header tank. And remember – you don't have to do the whole lot in one go.

CHOOSING A PUMP FOR A STREAM

A submersible pump is quite powerful enough to run a stream up to 6m (20ft) long. It must be placed in the lowest point of the bottom pond. When choosing a pump, measure the difference in height between the top of the upper pond and the top of the lower pond, as you'll need this information to use in conjunction with the maker's information on the side of the box. Take the width of the waterfall chute into account too: for every 10cm (4in) of spill, you need 910/1135 litres, (200/250 gallons) per hour.

1 Begin by marking out the project – the stream should be a naturally flowing shape, running down a very slight slope and into the lower pond. Dig out the lower pond: it should be at least twice the size of the fibreglass shell that will form the upper pond. Line with sand and butyl, as on page 32.

2 To make the stream, dig out the channel, leaving some level places with slightly 'dished' areas in them to hold water when the pump is switched off.

3 Line the stream with damp soft sand and lay PVC liner inside – the stream liner should overlap the liner in the lower pond. Pave round the edge of the lower pond (see page 29).

Render the stream with mortar (3 parts sand to 1 part cement) and, while it is wet, push in rocks to make a natural surface and leave to dry. You will then need to seal the stream bed. Read the instructions on the liquid resin sealant to find out how long you should leave the mortar on the stream bed before it is dry enough for you to paint it.

4 Dig out and install the upper pond, using a preformed pond shell as described on page 45. To make the chute, cut a 7.5cm- (3in-)wide and 2.5cm (1in-)deep notch out of the edge of the pool. Use a fibreglass car-

repair kit to build up the edges of the notch to make a lip with sides that funnel the water into the stream, as a mini waterfall. Alternatively use more fibreglass to seal the lip down on to a rock, so the water cascades down over 'rapids'. The header pond must be absolutely level or the water will run out on one side.

5 Lay on the electricity supply as described on page 14. Place the pump in the lowest part of the lower pond. Lay 2.5cm- (1in-)diameter hosepipe from the pump to the upper pond, making sure that it is concealed.

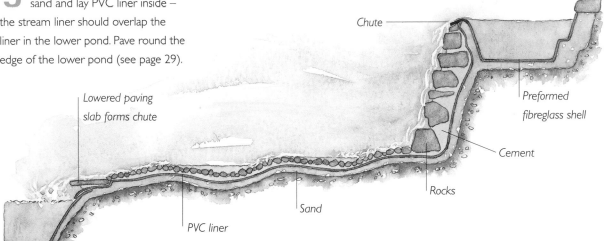

Chute

Lowered paving slab forms chute

Preformed fibreglass shell

Cement

Rocks

Sand

PVC liner

CHARLIE'S NOTEBOOK

charlie's top water garden plants

MARGINALS

Marginal plants stand on planting shelves round the edge of the pond. For a small pond, choose compact kinds, like those listed here. Cut back marginals close to the top of the pot in the autumn, and at other times of year if they look tatty, to encourage healthy, new growth.

Acorus gramineus 'Variegatus'
(variegated Japanese rush)
Height 38cm (15in); spread 30cm (1ft); depth 0–10cm (0–4in)
Great for a grassy look, very variegated and compact, needs splitting only every four years. Evergreen, but tatty by autumn, so best cut back then.

Caltha palustris 'Plena'
Height 15cm (6in); spread 30cm (1ft); depth 0–10cm (0–4in)
One of the first spring flowers, making compact hummocks, with double, buttercup-yellow flowers, and it often blooms again late in the year. Divide every three to four years.

TOP: Equisetum hyemale.

RIGHT: Carex elata *'Aurea' (Bowles golden sedge)*.

Carex elata 'Aurea'
(Bowles golden sedge)
Height 60cm (2ft); spread 45cm (1½ft); depth 0–12.5cm (0–5in)
Forms a shaggy, roundish clump of bright yellow foliage, with black seedheads that look stunning in spring.

Equisetum hyemale
Height 60cm (2ft); spread 45cm (1½ft); depth 0–18cm (0–7in)
Tall, thick, tubular, green leaves with black, horizontal stripes that make it look like a bamboo. Related to horsetail, but slow-growing and looks fabulous.

Houttuynia cordata 'Plena'
Height 23cm (9in); spread 30cm (1ft); depth 0–12.5cm (0–5in)
Dark green, heart-shaped leaves with red edges and pretty, double, pink-flecked white flowers. Grows as a neat clump in a pond; spreads in a bog garden. Late to emerge.

Iris laevigata (Japanese water iris)
Height 45–60cm (1½–2ft); spread 45cm (1½ft); depth 0–12.5cm (0–5in)
Three-cornered, dark blue iris flowers and strappy leaves; not for very small ponds. Flowers for about two weeks.

Iris laevigata 'Variegata'
(variegated Japanese water iris)
Height 50cm (20in); spread 60cm (2ft);
depth 0–12.5cm (0–5in)
The essential iris. The stripy, fan-shaped
foliage looks good all season and keeps
its stripes, unlike many.

Iris versicolor
Height 60cm (2ft); spread 60cm (2ft);
depth 0–12.5cm (0–5in)
Lots of smaller, strong purple flowers
with a yellow fleck in the centre on a
staggered stem; daintier than other
marginal irises.

Juncus effusus 'Spiralis' (corkscrew rush)
Height 45cm (1½ft); spread 30cm (1ft);
depth 0–10cm (0–4in)
Spiralling leaves that are evergreen in
the mildest areas. Not too vigorous; split
regularly to keep the leaves spiralling.

Lobelia 'Queen Victoria'
Height 75cm (2½ft); spread 30cm (1ft);
depth 0–10cm (0–4in)
Purple foliage and scarlet flowers in
late summer. Not a long-lived
perennial, nor reliably hardy – safest
grown with 10cm (4in) of water over
the crown. In a really cold area, move it
under cover in winter.

Myosotis scorpioïdes 'Mermaid'
(water forget-me-not)
Height 30cm (1ft); spread 30cm (1ft);
depth 0–10cm (0–4in)
More compact version of water forget-
me-not, with a long flowering season.
Cut back if it gets mildewy.

TOP: Iris laevigata *(Japanese water iris).*
ABOVE: Pontederia cordata *(pickerel weed).*
RIGHT: Zantedeschia aethiopica *(arum lily).*

Pontederia cordata (pickerel weed)
Height 60cm (2ft); spread 60cm (2ft);
depth 0–12.5cm (0–5in)
Glossy, heart-shaped leaves and tall
spikes of blue flowers; a lovely
structural plant for a formal pond.

Scirpus zebrinus (zebra rush)
Height 75cm (2½ft); spread 45cm
(1½ft); depth 0–15cm (0–6in)
Striped, reedy foliage. Loses its stripes
after two to three years; to restore
them, split and repot it.

Typha minima (miniature bulrush)
Height 60cm (2ft); spread 30cm (1ft);
depth 0–10cm (0–4in)
Like a miniature bulrush, with very
fine foliage and pompom seedheads.
To make it flower, don't cut hard
back in autumn, and leave it to get
potbound.

Zantedeschia aethiopica (arum lily)
Height 75cm (2½ft); spread 45cm
(1½ft); depth 0–20cm (0–8in)
Pure white flowers with big, bold,
succulent-looking foliage that makes
large clumps. Quite hardy if you grow
it with 20cm (8in) of water over it.

DEEP-WATER AQUATICS, OXYGENATORS AND FLOATERS

These are the plants that grow under, in or on the water. If you have fish, oxygenators are a 'must'. But in any pond, plants whose leaves or whole bodies float on the water are invaluable for providing shade, without which the whole pond eco-system goes wrong.

Deep-water Aquatics

Stand these on the floor of the pond; some kinds spread out over the water surface, while others grow up out of the water.

Aponogeton distachyos (water hawthorn)
Spread 38cm (15in); depth 25–75cm (10in–2½ft)
A good alternative to water lilies, ideal for small ponds. It has unusual, white flowers with a vanilla scent that is especially powerful in the evening.

Menyanthes trifoliata (bog bean)
Height 23cm (9in); spread 45cm (1½ft); depth 15–38cm (6–15in)
Spikes of pink-flecked white flowers with fluffy stamens in spring. Its roots stay in their basket while the stems spread out over the surface of the water. Vigorous native, but easily controlled.

Orontium aquaticum (golden club)
Height 30cm (1ft); spread 45cm (1½ft); depth 15–45cm (6in–1½ft)
Yellow, candle-like flowers in spring. The blue-green leaves appear later; some stick up and some lie down flat on the water. Though this plant will grow in shallower water, it won't flower well there.

Peltandra virginica
Height 75cm (2½ft); spread 45cm (1½ft); depth 10–45cm (4in–1½ft)
Striking, tropical-looking hardy plant with big, arrowhead leaves and small,

ABOVE: Orontium aquaticum *(golden club)*.

green, arum lily flowers good standing on an upturned basket in the middle of the pond.

Oxygenators

Elodea is often sold as loose strands with a weight at the end; in a mature pond just drop them in – they root into the sediment on the bottom. In a new pond, and with other oxygenators, plant into pond baskets.

Callitriche verna (water starwort)
Pretty, native, evergreen plant forming light green rosettes on the water surface. A good, non-rampant oxygenator, ideal for a small pond.

LEFT: Peltandra virginica.

Elodea crispa/Lagarosiphon major
Common 'waterweed' with short, round, crispy foliage. It is easy and reliable. Vigorous but easily thinned as it comes out in handfuls; essential for any pond 1.8 × 1.5m (6 × 5ft) or larger.

Hottonia palustris (water violet)
One of the prettiest oxygenators there is, with ferny foliage and spikes of pink-lilac flowers that stick out 15cm (6in) above the water in spring. Non-rampant and ideal for small ponds, but wait till the pond has matured for two years before introducing it.

BELOW: Hottonia palustris *(water violet) is one of the few flowering oxygenators.*

Myriophyllum spicatum (milfoil)
Attractive, feathery foliage, but needs soft water and can be tricky, so you may have to reintroduce it several times before it succeeds. *M. proserpinacoïdes* (parrot's feather) is sometimes sold as an oxygenator, but actually grows out above the surface of the water.

Floaters

These just drift about on the surface of the water. To plant, simply drop them in. Choose hardy ones. If you want to grow water lettuce, water hyacinth and water chestnut, treat them as annuals unless growing them in a tank of water in a warm conservatory.

ABOVE: *An attractive and unusual plant,* Stratiotes aloïdes *(water soldier) grows best in medium to larger-sized ponds where its spiky foliage can be seen to advantage.*

Hydrocharis morsus-ranae (frogbit)
Looks like a tiny water lily with fat, kidney-shaped leaves and neat, white flowers. It overwinters as resting buds that fall to the bottom of the pond in late summer, then pop up again next spring.

Stratiotes aloïdes (water soldier)
An odd plant that looks like a pineapple, which is fun because it sinks in the winter and floats in the summer. It has 'babies' on the end of stalks, like a spider plant. Buy a plant with some roots dangling down from the base, or it is unlikely to survive.

85

water lilies

Choose easy, free-flowering varieties and make sure you buy ones that are the right size for your pond to avoid problems later. Small varieties of water lily take time to get established, so expect only occasional flowers for their first two summers. Give each a sachet of special water lily fertilizer as a 'booster'. After that they should flower continuously all summer. Miniatures have a shorter flowering season (June–September), but the bigger varieties will flower up till the first proper frost. And don't keep splitting them – this will not need doing for six or seven years.

Water lilies come in a good range of colours, but there are no varieties with deep yellow flowers, only soft yellow. Red water lilies have pale or even white flowers the first year you plant them: the true colour does not appear until they are well established.

Miniature: for a container or pond under 1–1.2m (3–4ft)

Nymphaea pygmaea 'Helvola'
Spread 30cm (1ft); depth 23–38cm (9–15in)
Speckled leaves, with lemon-yellow flowers. Like all miniature water lilies, this does not start flowering until late May or June, but then flowers continuously till September.

RIGHT: Nymphaea pygmaea *'Helvola'*.

Above: Nymphaea *'Gonnère'.*

Small: for a 1.2–1.5m (4–5ft) pond

Nymphaea candida
Spread 45–60cm (1½–2ft); depth
45–60cm (1½–2ft)
A traditional white flower with a
yellow centre, and apple-green leaves.

Nymphaea 'Froebeli'
Spread 60cm (2ft); depth 45–60cm
(1½–2ft)
A superb variety with lots of red, star-
shaped flowers about 7.5cm (3in) in
diameter; a three-year-old plant will
have around twelve blooms open at
once.

Medium: for a 1.8–2.4m (6–8ft) pond

Nymphaea odorata 'William B. Shaw'
Spread 1–1.2m (3–4ft); depth
60–75cm (2–2½ft)
Big, 'girlie', pale pink flowers, 12.5cm
(5in) across, which bleach to blush-
white two days after opening. The new
leaves are a very dark red, turning
greeny red with a slightly wavy edge.

Nymphaea 'Gonnère'
Spread 60cm–1m (2–3ft); depth
45–60cm (1½–2ft)
Nicknamed 'Snowball', this is a choice
white with double flowers that never
quite open, giving the impression of
snowballs floating in the water – not
many of them, but spectacular.

Large: for a pond 3m (10ft) and larger

Nymphaea 'Escarboucle'
Spread 1.5m (5ft); depth 1.2–1.4m
(4–4½ft)
Huge, dark scarlet flowers more than
15cm (6in) across and massive leaves
30–38cm (12–15in) wide make this a
water lily for only a really big pond, but it
is stunning.

Water Lily Problems

Water lily aphids *You probably see
this pest only one year in five, but it
makes the leaves look very tatty. Pick
off the worst ones, then hose the
aphids off the remaining leaves for
fish to eat. Clear up and destroy all
dead leaves in autumn to prevent
reinfestation next year.*

Water lily beetles *Brown beetles
1cm (½in) long, and black grubs like
ladybird larvae that eat water lily
leaves. Don't use pesticides in or near
water, but pick off the grubs by hand
or sink the leaves under the water so
that fish can feed on the larvae.*

RIGHT: Nymphaea *'Escarboucle'.*

fish and wildlife

FISH

To many people, a pond is not complete without fish. But though the pond is vital to the fish, fish are not vital to the pond. To maintain the right ecological balance, choose the correct sort of fish and keep no more than the pond can support.

Goldfish are my first choice for a small pond. They are colourful, friendly, and keep the pond clean. Shubunkins look similar to goldfish but with piebald markings, and Sarasa Comets are glamorous red and white fish with long, flowing tails. In a small pond avoid koi and other kinds of carp. They grow far too big and wreck your plants.

If you decide to have fish, you must also have oxygenating plants For a small pond use compact oxygenators like water violet or starwort— even though they die down in winter, there is still enough oxygen in the water for the fish.

TOP: *In spring, frogs are likely to seek out your pond to lay their spawn.*

RIGHT: *Goldfish are ideal for a small pond. Avoid carp – they look beautiful but grow very large.*

You must also have a pond that is at least 60cm (2ft) deep over one-third of its area. The deeper water stays cool in hot weather and won't freeze in winter.

To calculate the right number of fish your pond can support, the magic formula is 2.5cm (1in) of fish – including the tail – per 0.09 metre (1 square foot) of pond surface. It is best to buy fish over 5cm (2in) long as smaller ones have a high mortality rate after being moved. When you have set up a new pond, wait two or three weeks before introducing fish while the oxygenators take root. Float the bag of fish for twenty to thirty minutes on the surface of the pond, then open it and let some pond water in, and five minutes later tip the bag over and let the fish swim out. Don't feed fish for the first few days as they'll be too nervous to eat.

Feeding

The main reason for feeding fish is that it makes them friendly. If you feed them once a day, at the same time and place, they will soon be waiting for you. Use good-quality (that is, expensive) feed: flakes for fish under 5cm (2in); feed pellets or sticks for ones with bigger mouths. However, you don't have to feed. In a healthy pond there is enough natural food – you can certainly go away on holiday without arranging a fish-sitter. In fact, fish make themselves useful by feeding on mosquito larvae. However, even if you don't normally feed, it is a good idea to do so in autumn and spring so that they put on weight and build up their strength

ABOVE: *Introducing goldfish to a new pond.*

before and after the winter. Avoid overfeeding as it pollutes the pond and creates a problem with algae.

WILDLIFE

Grass snakes These come for a swim but don't stay long. Leave them alone, they look beautiful.

Kingfishers You are very lucky if you get these. They mainly take small fish fry which need thinning out anyway.

Frogs There's no need to stock a pond with frogspawn or tadpoles: any adults in the neighbourhood will find it. (It's a complete myth that frogs return only to the pond in which they grew up to breed.)

Toads These visit the pond only to breed – they don't hang around like frogs do. They produce long thin strands of spawn wound around water plants.

Newts These don't normally appear until the pond has been in existence for three years or longer. They are very shy and secretive and like a pond that is not disturbed too much.

Herons

Herons are the number one enemy of fishponds. Besides catching and eating healthy fish, they injure others which die later. They are most troublesome in spring when they have young to feed, not in winter. They are no longer fooled by fake 'decoy' herons. Deter them by putting a 'trip-wire' round the pond or using an electronic heron alert, or cover the pond with a net. Herons are less of a problem in towns or where a pond is close to tall fences, a shed or a greenhouse, as they need a long, shallow flight path before landing.

water garden troubleshooter

Q My pond looks like pea soup. How can I make the water clear again?

A The water turns green because of the presence of microscopic algae, caused by too much sunlight and nutrients getting into the pond. A new pond takes three seasons to settle down, after which the plants will do the work for you by taking up nutrients and shading the surface. If you can't wait, use a filter. Older ponds often go green temporarily in spring before plants that die down in winter regrow. Green water also happens if you are overfeeding your fish or keep topping up the pond with tap water, which contains a lot of nutrients. Use a treatment only as a last resort, and then use a natural one that works by increasing the level of beneficial bacteria, which is what clears the pond.

RIGHT: *Duckweed may look attractive at first, but it quickly spreads, smothering floating and submerged plants. Adding a fountain is a great way of solving this problem as not only will it look good, but duckweed hates moving water and will be kept at bay.*

Q How do I get rid of blanket weed?

A The good news is that if you have blanket weed, you won't have green water. Like algae, it is the result of excess nutrients in the water. There are several chemical treatments (algicides), but they are a bit self-defeating, since when the blanket weed is killed it decomposes in the water and releases its nutrients back into the pond – ready to feed the next crop of blanket weed. Strong algicides can also kill off your water lilies and oxygenators if wrongly used. One good tip, if you have a waterfall, is to grow watercress in it. This acts like a vegetable filter to the water running through. The watercress takes up the nutrients and, so long as you keep harvesting the watercress (it's quite OK to eat), you slowly starve the blanket weed out. For a quick fix, just grab handfuls of blanket weed, pull it out and put it on the compost heap.

RIGHT: *Natural pools will attract wildlife and are one of the easiest types to make and maintain.*

Q Do snails help prevent algae or blanket weed?

A No. The commonest water snails, freshwater whelks, eat your plants too. Ramshorn snails are better for ponds as they mainly eat decomposing vegetation and algae. And tadpoles also feed on the spring flush of algae. But they are not going to fix the problem on their own.

Q How many plants do I need for my pond?

A Three plants per square metre (yard) of surface area is a good general rule. Aim to cover half to two-thirds of the surface of your pond with floating plants like water lilies and bog bean or golden club, and half the base of the pond with oxygenators by year three. (Don't count marginals in this, as the amount of shade they cast on the pond surface is negligible.) And don't plant thickly to start with or you will soon be pulling out waterweeds in armfuls.

Q Can you give me any tips on how to get rid of duckweed?

A Duckweed cuts out light completely, killing off the plants and in turn most of the waterlife. try to avoid an infestation by dunking new plants in a bucket of water to wash any

duckweed off before putting them into the pond. If you already have the problem, lift out all your plants and rinse them, then put a hosepipe into the pond and let it overflow so that the duckweed gets washed out. Scoop out any that is left using a net. Alternatively try putting in a fountain – duckweed hates moving water. There is also an algicide specially for duckweed (you need to use several doses), but I'd try other means first.

Q Can you give me a 'recipe' for a pond for a smallish garden?

A A nice size for the pond would be about 2.75 × 1.8m × 46–60cm deep (9 × 6ft × 1½–2ft deep). Add two medium or three small

water lilies, ten to fifteen bunches or pots of oxygenators, at least eight marginals and ten to fifteen ramshorn snails and, after a few weeks, put in ten 5–7.5cm (2–3in) fish — they will grow to 12.5–15cm (5–6in).

Q My water lily flowers don't last long – what is wrong?

A Three to four days is about the normal life of a water lily flower. When you start growing young plants, they have only one or two flowers out at a time, so you tend to notice them dying more. But by the time plants are three or four years old they have so many flowers open at once that you do not notice each one dying off as it is replaced so quickly.

RIGHT: *Planting rockery plants along the banks of the rocky cascade (see page 76). Creeping plants are great for features like this as they will gradually spread over the surrounding rocks and pebbles and make the feature look natural and established.*

Q I keep finding yellow leaves, or leaves with brown fringes or patches, round the outskirts of clumps of water lilies. Is this a disease?

A No, it's perfectly natural for the plant to dispense with the outer leaves after they are about a month old, as fresh new ones grow from the centre of the plant. Again, it is most noticeable on young plants since they have only a few leaves at a time. But once they are established each plant should grow enough leaves for you not to notice this gradual turnover.

Q My water lilies are not growing many new leaves. What's wrong?

A It could be several things. If you've used an algicide, check the instructions as some are not safe to use with water lilies. In this case, run half the water out of the pond and refill it to dilute the product more. If the plants have not been divided for seven years or more, divide them next spring. Lift them out of the pond, divide them and repot the best bit into aquatic soil. If neither of the above possibilities seems likely, the plant is probably short of nutrients, so give it a sachet of water lily fertilizer.

Q I want to have a big pond, and since the garden is on clay soil I'd like to save the cost of the liner by puddling the clay to make it hold water. How do I do it?

A This very rarely works. If you want a pond that will not leak, I'd strongly advise you to use a liner. However, if you fancy a try, I'd suggest making a small test pond first to see if your clay type is suitable. Dig a small 'puddle' about 60cm (2ft) deep and the same across. As you dig down, check that you don't dig through the clay layer into a porous type of soil further down. Put 2.5cm (1in) or so of water in the bottom, then get in with your wellies on and squelch around in it for a bit. Take some more clay and smear it over the surface of the trampled mud, in much the same way as a plasterer skims a wall, leaving a smooth surface. (When you make the real pond, buy a special

clay product called Bentomat containing sodium bentonite, which has extra waterproofing power for this job, and cover it with a 15cm (6in) layer of soil afterwards.) Then fill the depression with water before the clay dries out and cracks. Leave the test pool for a few days to see if it holds water and, if all is well, go ahead with your full-sized pond.

Q What can I plant along the edge of a natural stream to stabilize the banks?

A One of the best plants for this job is *Onoclea sensibilis* (sensitive fern). The roots spread out over the side of the bank and hold it in place. It is an attractive, non-rampant plant and is happy growing in sun where the soil stays damp. *Darmera peltata* works quite well too, as its fat rhizomes mat together well. Dogwoods are also good.

Q Why do my tadpoles keep disappearing?

A Late frosts can wipe out a complete 'crop'. Frog tadpoles also have lots of natural predators. Birds, water snails, fish, dragonfly larvae and diving beetles all feed on them, as do fish – golden orfe are particularly bad in this respect, though goldfish hardly touch them. Toad tadpoles on the other hand are quite safe as they taste horrible. (Don't ask me how I know – I just do!)

BELOW: Onoclea sensibilis *(sensitive fern). Its spreading roots make it a good choice for stabilising stream banks.*

Q My pond liner sometimes balloons up out of the pond, coming right out above the surface of the water. Why is this and what do I do about it?

A This can happen when you build a pond on a site with a naturally high water table. When the level of underground water rises after a wet winter, it lifts the liner with it. If you have a butyl liner, which is flexible, it just drops back into place when the water table drops. But fibreglass liners, being rigid, don't 'give' at all and can crack or even pop right out of the ground. The moral of the story is: don't make a pond where there is a high water table. But if you must, make a raised one.

Q I think my pond is leaking. How can I mend it?

A Don't confuse natural evaporation with a leak: in hot or windy weather the water level can drop 5cm (2in) per week, or more if wind blows water from a fountain on to the surrounding garden. If the level drops faster than this or continues falling in winter, suspect a leak.

1 If you have a waterfall, turn the pump off and see if the water level drops. The cascade part is where 99 per cent of leaks occur.
2 Don't top the pond up – let the water level keep dropping. When it stops, the leak will be found on the water-line – often the planting shelf.
3 If the level drops quickly, you have a big hole. Look for a wet patch of soil just outside the pond.
4 When you find the hole in a pond with a liner, fixing it is like mending a puncture on a bicycle. You don't need to empty the pond totally. Just bale it out a bit, let the liner dry out for twenty-four hours, then clean the area up and stick a pond repair patch on, following the maker's directions. A fibreglass pond can be mended using a fibreglass car-repair kit.
5 If you can't locate the hole, the only thing to do is take everything out of the pond, lay a new liner over the top of the old one and start again.

If a new pond leaks right from the start, check to see if a fold in the liner is acting as a lip which water can run over. Adjusting this will stop it in seconds.

useful addresses

Most of the basic equipment you will need can be found in your local water garden centre. However, if you find it difficult to get hold of more specialist materials, the following suppliers may be able to help.

Blagdon Water Gardens
Bath Road
Upper Langford
North Somerset BS18 7DN
Tel. 01934 852973

Chenies Aquatics Ltd
The Van Hage Garden Company
Chenies
Near Rickmansworth
Hertfordshire WD3 6EN
Tel. 01494 764 549

Erin-Gardena
(for garden lighting)
Astonia House
High Street
Baldock
Hertfordshire SG7 6PP
Tel. 01462 896 989

Hozelock Ltd
Waterslade House
Thame Road
Haddenham
Aylesbury
Buckinghamshire HP17 8JD
Tel. 01844 292 002

Interpet
Interpet House
Vincent Lane
Dorking
Surrey RH4 3YX
Tel. 01306 881033

Lotus Water Garden Products Ltd
(for self-contained water features and ornaments)
Junction Street
Burnley
Lancashire BB12 0NA
Tel. 01282 420 771

Mill Water Gardens
Mill Lane
Romsey
Hampshire SO51 8ER
Tel. 01794 513 444

Oase UK
(for pumps and pond lighting)
3 Telford Gate, Whittle Road
West Portway Industrial Estate
Andover, Hampshire SP10 3SF
Tel. 01264 333225

Queenswood Garden Centre
(for pebble pools, pumps and fountains)
Wellington
Hereford HR4 8BB
Tel. 01432 830 015

Solar Solutions Fountains
(for solar-powered equipment)
6 High Street
Kington, Herefordshire HR5 3AX
Tel. 01544 230 303

Stapeley Water Gardens
London Road
Stapeley
Nantwich, Cheshire CW5 7LH
Tel. 01270 623868

Tetra
Lambert Court
Chestnut Avenue
Eastleigh, Hampshire SO53 3ZQ
Tel. 01703 620 500

index

PICTURE REFERENCES

BBC Books would like to thank the following for providing photographs and for permission to reproduce copyright material. While every effort has been made to trace and acknowledge all copyright holders, we would like to apologize should there have been any errors or omissions.

BBC Worldwide 4b, 8L, 15t, 19L, 28t, 49, 50, 52, 54, 64, 66, 72, 81L (Susan Bell), 19r, 31, 81r (Craig Easton), 15b, 12t, 53 (BBC Gardeners' World Magazine), 4m, 5b, 16t, 20r, 22, 30, 35, 36, 56, 60r, 68, 69 (John Glover), 2, 4t, 5m, 7, 9r, 11, 12b, 14, 17, 18L, 18/19, 23, 25, 26, 27, 33, 58, 61, 63, 67, 70L, 73, 76, 78, 81r, 89 (Tim Sandall).

Ardea 57, 93; Dave Bevan 41t; Pat Brindley 46L; The Garden Picture Library 8r (Howard Rice), 13 (Kim Blaxland), 18r (Howard Rice), 21 (Lamontagne), 24 (Howard Rice), 40 (Sunniva Harte), 41b (Gary Rogers), 42 (Sunniva Harte), 44 (John Glover), 47 (Geoff Dann), 59r (Lamontagne), 80r (J S Sira), 82t (Jerry Pavia), 83t (Clive Nichols), 83m (J S Sira), 83b (Steve Wooster), 84t (John Glover), 84b (Eric Crichton), 85t (Mayer/Le Scanff), 86 (Howard Rice), 87b (Mayer/Le Scanff), 88t (Sunniva Harte), 88b (Ron Sutherland), 90 (Steve Wooster), 91 (Bob Challinor); Garden/Wildlife Matters 16b, 38; John Glover Photography 5t, 20L, 39, 59L, 60L, 62, 74L, 80L; Harpur Garden Picture Library 70r, 75; Andrew Lawson Photography 28, 46t; Planet Earth Pictures 80/81, 85b; Photos Horticultural 71; Stapeley Water Gardens Ltd 29, 74r; Jo Whitworth 9L, 8/9, 10, 55, 82b, 87t.